MW01680665

Pocket Sponsor®

24/7 'Back to the Basics'
Support for Addiction Recovery

The Original Pocket Sponsor®
From those who brought you *Day By Day*

The Original Pocket Sponsor Series
Day By Day

Pocket Sponsor®

First Edition, 2003
2nd Printing, 2004
3rd Printing, 2005

ISBN 0-9674915-2-5
Library of Congress Control Number: 2003103105

For information on the *Pocket Sponsor®*
www.pocketsponsor.com

For information on *Day By Day, Recovery Resources*
www.day-by-day.org

How to Use This Book

For the chemically dependent in recovery, this book is designed as a basic 24/7 form of support. There is nothing in here that you will not hear at meetings or that your sponsor wouldn't tell you. Now you can carry a little bit of fellowship with you wherever you go. How you begin your readings depends upon where you are.

If You are a Beginner (and those beginning again):

Start the readings immediately following your last drink, fix, or pill. Day One becomes your first day of abstinence.

Or start reading on the day you leave treatment. Day One is the day you are discharged.

For those with a few 24 Hours:

Use this book to correspond with the month you are in. Begin reading using today's date—is it the sixth? Then look up Day Six in the *Pocket Sponsor,* the time of day and read your message. Keep using it month after month—you will pick it up at different times and receive different recovery messages. Again and again you will discover new passages that are *exactly* what you need at that moment.

Back to the Basics

In beginning recovery, the *Pocket Sponsor* is meant to be carried with you at all times. For those of us with a few 24 hours, the *Pocket Sponsor* becomes a 24/7 'back to the basics' support that can be kept handy in our recovery library or on our bedside table. Although it has a message for every hour of every day, you need not read it every hour. When you arise in the morning and before retiring at night, it is a good habit to pull out the *Pocket Sponsor* and read the support passage. Anytime during the day that you feel uneasy, find the day and hour and read your message, especially during the HALT moments (too Hungry, Angry, Lonely, Tired).

The Realm of the Spirit

Whatever your Spiritual Source may be (God, Group, or Goodness), understand that this Pocket Sponsor uses the terms "God" as well as Allah, Buddha, Divine Intelligence and many other forms for a Supreme Being. We ascribe to the concept of using, as a foundation for recovery, a Power Greater than yourself and *of your understanding* as discussed in the Big Book of Alcoholics Anonymous,

> "To us, the Realm of the Spirit is broad, roomy, all inclusive; never exclusive or forbidding to those who earnestly seek. It is open, we believe to all men. When, therefore, we speak to you of God, we mean your own conception of God." (P46-47).

Don't let the God talk ever put you off—convert our terms to whatever works for you. Remember, nothing will work if you don't work it!

My recovery anniversary (abstinence birthday) is:

___

The name of my sponsor is:

___

My sponsor's phone number is:

___

The numbers of other support people are:

___

___

___

___

___

___

___

WEEK ONE

Day One/12:00 AM: Do not regret the past. "The past is but the beginning of a beginning/and all that is and has been/is but the twilight of the dawn." ~H. G. Wells from *Beside Prayers*. Your past is the beginning of this beginning.

I "will not regret the past nor wish to close the door on it." (P 83, AA Big Book)

Day One/1:00 AM: To earn respect, we must live responsibly. To live responsibly, we must identify and clarify our personal value system, then act on a daily basis in accordance with that value system.

Respect is for the respectable.

Day One/2:00 AM: If you think you are having a problem with God, just try to imagine the problem He/She is having with you!

There is no way to know God's Will unless I do it.

Day One/3:00 AM: Don't "should" on yourself. You "should" have done this, you "should" have done that, is not program. What you do *now*, is program.

Most "shoulds" are a lie.

Day One/4:00 AM: When we pray for strength, the Universe gives us difficulties to make us strong. When we pray for courage, the Universe gives us danger to overcome. When we pray for patience, the Universe gives us long lines and traffic jams. What are you praying for?

I may ask for favors but the Universe gives me opportunities.

Day One/5:00 AM: Wet the bed and blame the blanket—that is the life we led. With the Twelve Steps, we learn that problems are basically of our own making.

At the end of BLAME is ME.

Day One/6:00 AM: We remain recovered as long as we remain recovering. We never become drink and drug proof.

In order to remain successful in this program,
I remember that I AM a verb—present tense.

Day One/7:00 AM: They say there are three answers to every prayer: "Yes," "No," and "Not Now." And when waiting, remember that The Universe doesn't wear a watch.

Patience means that I give God space.

Day One/8:00 AM: We used to live to the dictates of that first fix, pill, drink, smoke, or snort. In our new life, we live to the dictates of a higher law. It is our most challenging task. What does it take? All you have.

Working my program and staying clean and sober may take all that I have, but I have all that it takes.

Day One/9:00 AM: We used to cope with life instinctually using drugs—reacting to everything by reaching for the mood-elevators, crack, weed, and booze. Today we learn to be proactive, not reactive. We learn to respond (with thought and deliberation) rather then react (instinctually).

I do not "react" but "respond" to the situations in my life. I "think" rather than "drink" my way through issues.

Day One/10:00 AM: "This time, like all times, is a very good one if we but know what to do with it." ~Ralph Waldo Emerson. Every thought you have can be part of a continuous prayer and everything you do can be your practice of healing.

If I'm not happy today, what am I waiting for?

Day One/11:00 AM: Responsible. This word is a combination of "response" and "able." When you want to know who is responsible for something, ask yourself who is "able" to "respond." That is your answer.

Responsibility is simply my response to God's ability.

Day One/12:00 PM: You can't change reality but you can change your attitude toward it.

When reality messes up my fantasies, I pause and ask my Higher Power to guide my thoughts.

Day One/1:00 PM: There are times when we don't like ourselves very well. Consequently, we usually don't like others too well either. But we can grant others this: The right to be human, the right to be wrong, and the right to be right!

When people really bug me, let me let them be.

Day One/2:00 PM: Are you going to let tough times make you bitter or make you better?

I embrace "tough" times because I get to practice my principles.

Day One/3:00 PM: "There are more things in heaven and earth... than are dreamt of in your philosophy." ~William Shakespeare. Hold on to the knowledge that more good is occurring on this hunk of rock floating through space than you can ever imagine.

I ask for all things that I might enjoy life, I am given life that I might enjoy all things.

Day One/4:00 PM: Remember, if you have ten problems and pick up, you'll then have eleven!

I remember that I am only one drink away from a drunk and one hit away from a high.

Day One/5:00 PM: Seemingly "bad" days are usually the days in which we don't get our own way. This is a Third Step problem. If you are having a "bad" day, read the

Third Step from your basic recovery text and ask yourself what part of your life today has not been turned over.

Today I work toward matching my will to my Higher Power's, not my Higher Power's to mine.

Day One/6:00 PM: Gaining our strength in recovery by admitting our powerlessness in addiction is a mystery to us. But, the First Step says we are powerless over "our drug of choice" and not powerless over "our recovery." Don't limit yourself.

I am powerfully recovering.

Day One/7:00 PM: There is no right way to do the wrong thing. Whatever you were thinking of doing, you can not rationalize it into "right" action by saying, "yes but this" or "no but that." You know what's right and you know what's wrong—that gut feeling guides you.

When things go wrong, I don't go with them.

Day One/8:00 PM: They say that there is no elevator to peace of mind, *we must use the Steps*. All the Steps ask us to do is trust God, clean house, and serve others. We can do it. Just put Step One in front of the others and begin.

Which Step am I on today?

Day One/9:00 PM: Service is sacred. "…our sometimes smoke-filled, coffee-filled, talk-filled clubs, meetings, and social gatherings are the basis for a lot more than laughter—they add up to a major part of our recovery." May 29, *Day By Day*

Am I contributing to the fellowship?

Day One/10:00 PM: Meditation is a healthy activity that will strengthen not only your recovery but rejuvenate you physically and mentally as well. Prayers and meditation have been proven to strengthen the immune system.

In Step Eleven, I send a message of life to my immune

system as well as my spirit when I seek conscious contact with my Divine Source.

Day One/11:00 PM: We always have the choice to drink and drug again, until we drink and drug again. Then we have no choice.

I don't pick up even if my ass falls off!

§

Day Two/12:00 AM: If you are looking for the perfect group before you join a home group, then you are going to be homeless.

My home group members are not perfect and neither am I, so we suit each other perfectly.

Day Two/1:00 AM: It's hard to believe that this simple program can work for us. But it does. We see it each time an old timer celebrates a birthday, a newcomer picks up a token, or a former skid row drunk reaches out to help an alcoholic doctor that has hit his first meeting in desperation. Believe.

I make believe until I can believe.

Day Two/2:00 AM: "God speaks to us in many ways at many times. If we are spiritually alert, we will know it when it happens. A stray thought occurs; we overhear a bit of conversation, a passage in something we are reading suddenly stands out—and we know we have connected." (March 13, *In God's Care*)

If I do not hear my Higher Power talking to me, it is because I am not listening.

Day Two/3:00 AM: Self will and 'running the show' can be like the monkey who sticks his hand into the trap for food. He grasps the food tightly creating a fist that won't slide out the trap door. The monkey struggles but *won't release the food* and he is trapped. Holding tight to your will and your way can be the fist that traps you.

I Let Go and Let God. What a relief.

Day Two/4:00 AM: Our program will work for people who believe in God. Our program will work for people who don't believe in God. Our program *will not work* for people who believe they are God.

*A God of my understanding, a God not of my understanding. God can simply be a "**G**roup **O**f **D**runks" if I choose!*

Day Two/5:00 AM: Us addicts are often hyper-vigilant about others "talking behind our backs" or slandering us. Our sponsors tell us that what "they" think of us is none of our business. It can still be hard to take.

It matters not if someone speaks badly of me; I live so no one will believe it.

Day Two/6:00 AM: It's a God thing. There are no co-incidences, they are God-incidences.

It was no accident that I found the Twelve Steps as an answer to my disease of addiction.

Day Two/7:00 AM: And so our very *best* thoughts won't save us. When we are given a program of action, it tells us what to DO, not what to think. Think anything you want, just DO the suggestions (*your thoughts will change*).

What can I do this moment to have an awesome day?

Day Two/8:00 AM: Many times we thought we used chemicals because we were unhappy, but nine times out of ten in coming to this program, we discovered "Better living through chemicals" is what made us unhappy!

I know that happiness comes from the inside out, not the outside in.

Day Two/9:00 AM: Think. Think. Think. It is *not thinking* that allows us to pick up a drink or a drug. If we think about what picking up really means, if we "Think a drink and a drug through" we won't be able to do it.

If I get hit by a train, it is not the caboose that kills me.

Day Two/10:00 AM: Everybody makes mistakes. Fools repeat them, the weak excuse them, only the wise admit and profit from them.

If I really want to find a solution to my current quandary, I will. If not, I will find an excuse.

Day Two/11:00 AM: "Thoroughly have we seen a person fail who has rarely followed our path." This is an interesting slip of the tongue from Chapter Five of *Alcoholic's Anonymous*. Yet it contains a lot of wisdom.

I cannot work the steps too soon, because I do not know how soon it may be too late.

Day Two/12:00 PM: Today you are leading a life. When you were drinking and drugging, you were a life being led.

It is God's job to make miracles and I am one of them.

Day Two/1:00 PM: Sometimes you won't believe that all is well. You'll think "Everything is shit and I don't want to hear others telling me it's OK." Alright, be angry *and* go to a meeting tonight and tell them it's not OK.

I'm not OK until I'm OK just like this.

Day Two/2:00 PM: When all else fails, read the AA Big Book (CDA First Edition or NA Basic Text).

I think I'll take the short cut and read it first.

Day Two/3:00 PM: "For a time we are living inside a scream where there seems to be no exit, only echoes. The small cares that seemed so important yesterday seem like nothing, and our daily concerns become petty and irrelevant. When we finally reclaim ourselves, as we ultimately do, we are changed." ~Kent Nerburn, *Simple Truths*

Cooperating with God is the easier softer way.

Day Two/4:00 PM: As our addiction struggles to maintain its power over us, it will present many false claims to pull us back into the mire of destruction. When you are in a meeting, your disease is in the parking lot doing push-ups.

My fear is not a fact. My FEAR is:
False Evidence Appearing Real

Day Two/5:00 PM: "Nothing contributes more to the peace of the soul than having no opinion at all." ~George Christopher Lichtenberg

When I have no opinion on outside issues, I cannot be drawn into controversy. (Tradition Ten)

Day Two/6:00 PM: You may have been trying to make the best of your pain. We ask you only to begin to learn to allow it to make the best of you.

If I share my pain I cut it in half, if I don't, I double it

Day Two/7:00 PM: You are an exceptional human being. There has never been anyone with your personality, ability, and unique way of seeing things. Take the world by storm because you have what it takes!

I used to feel impending doom. Now
I feel impending good.

Day Two/8:00 PM: You may feel like an emotional orphan at various times throughout your recovery. It's pretty normal for us. When feeling disconnected, try watchful breathing. Take a breath and watch it. Again. Again. This will help connect you to that place of belonging that resides within you.

I breathe in. I breathe out. I use my breath to still my sometimes frantic emotions. Then I call my sponsor.

Day Two/9:00 PM: Often the shadow of our addiction

falls across our good intentions. It is so hard to stay clean and sober at times. This is not a picnic for us. When it gets unbearable, ASK FOR HELP from a fellow recovering addict, your counselor, your pastor or your group!

The Divine gently nudges me to ask for help as I need it.

Day Two/10:00 PM: Let go or be dragged…

I pray for the willingness to be willing to be willing to let go absolutely. (P 97, Meeting Wisdom)

Day Two/11:00 PM: If having the right thoughts and desires were enough, we probably wouldn't need Twelve Step programs of action. Few of us had a shortage of good thoughts or high resolves when it came to controlling the use of mind affecting chemicals. And yet, when that craving hit, our minds so cleverly found an excuse to use "just this one more time" and our good thoughts went right down the toilet.

I can't think myself into right action, but must act myself into right thinking.

§

Day Three/12:00 AM: Egoism isn't necessarily thinking a lot of yourself--just thinking of yourself a lot.

I begin this day by thinking of another first. Who is distressed or frightened that I may offer words of comfort?

Day Three/1:00 AM: "Be humble and you will not stumble." A simple thought; a mighty message.

If I am not humble, I will be humiliated.

Day Three/2:00 AM: Rebellious alcoholic and addict personalities die hard. As you receive your tokens, marking your progress from one stage of recovery to the next, that little rebel in you sabotages your triumph: "This is stupid, don't embarrass yourself, you don't need these people..."

I am a token taker and the token in my pocket counters the rebel in my head.

Day Three/3:00 AM: When hurting, confused, or afraid, the smartest thing us chemical dependents can say is: I need HELP: **H**ope, **E**ncouragement, **L**ove, **P**atience.

I am the captain of my ship, but a captain needs a crew. I accept the help of others.

Day Three/4:00 AM: Witness the miracle of recovery happening for others, and you come to believe that this miracle can happen for you as well. Look at the miracles around you, one month off drugs, three years, 20 years or more. You are surrounded by living miracles.

I do not believe in miracles, I rely on them.

Day Three/5:00 AM: Many meetings, many chances; few meetings, few chances; no meetings, no chances.

The trouble with staying home and isolating is I get a lot of bad advice.

Day Three/6:00 AM: Effective recovery means changing just about everything you used to be comfortable with: your playmates, your hangouts, maybe even your job. Sometimes it's easy, sometimes not so easy, but change we must.

When I accept change, the possibilities are infinite.

Day Three/7:00 AM: "Once having understood, you should read the teachings of the sages many times." ~Dogen, *The Pocket Zen Reader.* Read the AA Big Book and other basic texts over and over. You will be amazed at how they keep changing!

It is amazing how much I learn after I think I know it already.

Day Three/8:00 AM: If something is right, it can be

done. If it is wrong, it can be done without.

I can do that!

Day Three/9:00 AM: Many times we thought we used chemicals because we were unhappy, but coming to this program, we discovered that using too many chemicals is what *made* us unhappy. Now is the time to break the old unhappy pattern.

My happiness is an inside job.

Day Three/10:00 AM: They say both, "My best thinking got me drunk" and "Think a drink through." Which is it? Are our thoughts friend or foe? Both, and the difference between "stink'n think'n" and "straight thinking" is simply self-honesty. We find a good place to start in Step Four.

I have to think everything I believe, but I don't have to believe everything I think.

Day Three/11:00 AM: Look. Listen. Learn. Look at the clean and sober people in the program. Listen to how they did it. Learn to apply it to you.

May I learn to listen and listen to learn.

Day Three/12:00 PM: Professionals and relatives express varied opinions about what you suffer from and why. Even people in our rooms express widely different opinions on alcoholism and addiction. As William Blake writes "Both read the Bible day and night, But thou read'st black where I read white." Never allow others to make you feel "less than" because you have this disease

I have a disease, not a disgrace.

Day Three/1:00 PM: Anger. "Anger" is one letter away from danger.

If I am right, I don't need to be angry. If I am wrong, I can't afford to be angry.

Day Three/2:00 PM: Take the "alcohol" out of the "alcoholic" and you're left with the "ic". Are you an untreated "ic?"

The Twelve Steps is how I treat the "ic" in me, the sick in me.

Day Three/3:00 PM: Every human being is a design of Divine Intention. The complex patterns of the universal cycles are not always understood, yet the world works so perfectly to sustain the cycles of life. You may not understand why you are chemically dependent, but rest assured there is a purpose in your cycle of sobriety.

I recognize the value of all Divine Intention, and trust in God's purpose for me.

Day Three/4:00 PM: Nothing happens by accident. There are no coincidences, they say, only God-incidences.

I believe that God can do for me what I can't do for myself. I believe in God-incidences.

Day Three/5:00 PM: Your history has no power over you. It has value, but no power. Your future has no power over you. It has value but no power. The only power of any importance in your life is the power of NOW.

I AM HERE NOW where the power is.

Day Three/6:00 PM: Now is a good time to stop and notice how the egg transforms into the chick, a caterpillar weaves his cocoon to emerge as a butterfly, and a seedling pushes up through the earth to meet the light of day. You realize that each of these steps is a different stage in a process of growth. You are involved in a process just as transforming.

My recovery is a process not an event.

Day Three/7:00 PM: When do you begin helping a newcomer? When you see a newcomer. Don't sweat it;

just do it.

When I work with a drunk, the drunk I'm working on is me.

Day Three/8:00 PM: Life on earth is one of polarity. We feel the comfort of love because we know the pain of rejection; we know the satisfaction of a full belly because we know the emptiness of hunger. Without darkness we can't appreciate the light; without cold we can't cherish the warmth. We know the joy of recovery because we came from the depths of despair.

I am not what I am in spite of my disease; I am what I am because of it.

Day Three/9:00 PM: From time immemorial mankind has sought to make outward appearances take the place of interior change. Don't try to fool others into thinking you are "together" before you really feel it, even if it would make them more comfortable. Don't be the guy or gal "whistling in the dark." (P 152, AA Big Book)

I know recovery is an inside job.

Day Three/10:00 PM: We find that the difference between adventure and disaster usually boils down to attitude. It's like the glass half full or half empty. Is it a problem or an opportunity; an obstruction or a challenge for growth? The way you choose to see it makes all the difference.

I don't see thing as they are, I see things as I am.

Day Three/11:00 PM: Practicing the principles can never be done from a pedestal of self-righteousness. The very act of judging, complaining or criticizing, demonstrates that we are spiritually out of whack--not the ones we judge. Oh, they may be out of whack too, but that's not our side of the street, is it?

My program does not work in principle.

It only works in practice.

§

Day Four/12:00 AM: Today is the tomorrow you worried about yesterday. The truth is that your Spiritual Source doesn't deal with time, clocks, and calendars. Your Source put you in today because your Source is in today.

Because God (Allah, Krishna, Kahuna, Creator, Divine Intelligence) is in the NOW, then 'Just for Today' I stay here too.

Day Four/1:00 AM: Worry is a control problem, because one worries only when something isn't going the way they want it to. The only reason to worry is because you don't have control over the outcome and don't trust your Higher Power.

Worry is like a rocking horse; it keeps me moving but never gets me anywhere.

Day Four/2:00 AM: Some recovering addicts take comfort in their complexity as if they are the exceptionally wounded. They worry their wounds and pick at their pain, giving themselves permission to be difficult, slow, and self-absorbed. Are you simply healing to your own internal rhythm or giving yourself excuses to be difficult?

I don't make the pity pot too comfortable.

Day Four/3:00 AM: Try to live your life without adding to your Eight Step list. You have enough wreckage to clear up from the past without creating wreckage in the now.

When I feel my worst, I try my best.

Day Four/4:00 AM: Yesterday is like a canceled check already spent. Tomorrow is a promissory note you do not have yet. Today is cash. Spend it wisely.

I begin my day with the Third Step Prayer, end my day with the Eleventh Step Meditation, and everything in-between is exactly as it should be.

Day Four/5:00 AM: When you work with others, you allow Divine Intelligence to speak and smile through you. You allow the Divine to reach out and hug the drunk, the junkie, and the dope head.

All people smile in the same language.

Day Four/6:00 AM: What we believed when we were five was not what we believed by the time we turned twelve. What we think we know at two years sobriety will change when we have eight. It is for this reason that we have "suggested" steps and not commandments.

Not only is the way I work the steps today different from the way others may work the steps today, but it may be different from the way I work them tomorrow!

Day Four/7:00 AM: Do not ask what your Higher Power can do for you, but rather what you can do for your Higher Power. This gets us out of self.

Dear God, what can I do for you today?

Day Four/8:00 AM: Even when it seems nothing is working right, *more is working right than not right.* Breathe. Your lungs work. Look across the room. Your eyes work. The sun is up. It works. Imagine the electrical, plumbing, telephone, and transportation systems in your city. In the larger picture, more is working than not working in your world.

It's a pretty good day, more things work then don't, and it'll stay a pretty good day as long as I don't make it worse.

Day Four/9:00 AM: Just when the caterpillar thinks the

world is coming to an end, God turns it into a butterfly.

I will not leave five minutes before the miracle happens.

Day Four/10:00 AM: God is always in today. Think about it. When it's 1 PM in New York, it's 11 AM in LA, and 8 PM in Hawaii. In Europe it's yesterday and in Australia it's tomorrow. If you try to get to the Europe to find yesterday, you will find today and should you jet yourself to Australia to find tomorrow, you will still end up in today. So actually it is "today" everywhere in the entire Universe!

When I have one foot in yesterday and the other in tomorrow, I am pissing on today.

Day Four/11:00 AM: The world does not always make sense. Not to the human mind, anyway. If you force facts to try and make sense when they don't, you drive yourself crazy. Sometimes the answer to questions like "Why? Why am I chemically dependent? Why me?" are unanswerable.

Even though I may never know exactly "Why?" I do know exactly HOW to address my chemical dependency.

Day Four/12:00 PM: People who seek a sponsor without faults, will be without a sponsor.

I know that my sponsor is willing to make mistakes, if I am willing to learn from them.

Day Four/1:00 PM: End your prayers with a Thank You, Thank You, Thank You!!! The first thank you is for what it was like. The second thank you is for what happened. And the third thank you is for what it is like now.

When I am grate-ful, I am grace-filled.

Day Four/2:00 PM: You are either *pro*gressing or *re*gressing. There is no such thing as standing still; there is no such thing as simply "gressing."

I can only coast one way, and that's downhill.

Day Four/3:00 PM: As a general rule, questions that ask "why" go in the wrong direction, seeking explanations that blame and shame. Questions that begin with "How" and "What" as in "How do I start my Fourth?" and "What can I learn from this?" lead to solutions, where the light bulb goes on in your head.

I ask questions that lead to exclamations not explanations.

Day Four/4:00 PM: Part of recovery is becoming whole and that includes relationships. But we must be a whole person seeking a whole person, not a broken person seeking another to become whole.

It's not a question of me finding the right person, but becoming the right person. (Especially if I'm already with someone!)

Day Four/5:00 PM: Sometimes you are the wind; sometimes you are the bug; sometimes you are the windshield.

Experience is what I get when I don't get what I want.

Day Four/6:00 PM: Depression is an emotion that fills the empty spaces where addiction used to live. It is natural to be depressed before we fill those spaces with our new life. Do not let people act as if your natural sadness means you are not working the program. If you were not sad, it would mean you do not seriously mean to give up your addiction.

When I find my life empty, I put program into it.

Day Four/7:00 PM: Our program of recovery teaches us progress, not perfection.

There may be people who expect me to be perfect, but because of the 12 Steps and my Higher Power,

I am not one of them.

Day Four/8:00 PM: Often the difference between a bad attitude and a good one is simply what you call it. You can be lonely or enjoy blessed solitude. You can be burdened or building strength. People can use you or you can be of use to others.

Whether it is AA for 'Altered Attitude,' NA for 'New Attitude,' or CDA for 'Change 'D Attitude,' my attitude today is a direct reflection of my personal growth.

Day Four/9:00 PM: "Rather than put a label on yourself as Christian, Jew, Moslem, Buddhist, or whatever, instead make a commitment to be Christ-like, God-like, Buddha-like and Mohammed-like." ~ Dr. Wayne Dryer

I make a commitment to be "Twelve Step-like" today.

Day Four/10:00 PM: Recovery is a Process Not an Event. There will never be a graduation day for your new way of life. The more you learn and grow the more you will see that you have more to learn and grow. That is what Steps Ten, Eleven, and Twelve are all about.

I learn to grow and grow to learn. My day of graduation is when I die.

Day Four/11:00 PM: When you are in the wrong place, the right place is empty.

Do I know my rightful place in recovery?

§

Day Five/12:00 AM: We may have the right to be wrong, but our steps teach us that we don't have the right to *do* wrong.

When my only reason for doing something is "because I have the right!" it usually turns out wrong.

Day Five/1:00 AM: We often hear "turn it over." This means turn over problems not under our control right now--whether they are with family, friends, work, or the law--we offer the things we cannot change to a Higher Power and LET GO.

If I turn it over and don't let go, I'll be upside down!

Day Five/2:00 AM: Often faith has been used as a weapon against us (or we used it against others), blaming our lack of recovery or progress on a lack of faith. If you are having trouble understanding faith right now, think about this: Faith is a tool, not a weapon.

I put down my weapons and pick up the tools.

Day Five/3:00 AM: "You should not be esteemed by others if you have no real inner virtue." ~Dogen, *The Pocket Zen Reader* You get esteem by doing something esteeming.

I never have to worry about low self-esteem when I do esteeming things.

Day Five/4:00 AM: Repression without expression, leads to depression. With a thorough Fourth Step, you *cannot* repress it. With a thorough Fifth Step, you get to express it.

Repression is my disease asking me to come out and play.

Day Five/5:00 AM: It is very important that we listen to what we are telling ourselves. What are the negatives? "This won't work; I wasn't so bad; my sponsor is sicker than me." You are the result of what you tell yourself.

I am the result of what I tell myself. What picture am I painting of myself today?

Day Five/6:00 AM: The safest banks fail, corporations fold, loved ones die, all things change. Your life now changes like the tides or the seasons. You are not alone in this change. Seek out others who have experienced relief from your problem of choice and let them guide you through it.

I can change my clothes and change my address but until I change myself, I cannot grow.

Day Five/7:00 AM: To aid you in working the Third Step, try taping this note onto your bathroom mirror for a week: "Good morning, this is your HP. I will not be needing your help today."

I STOP trying to run the show and
Start Turning Over Problems!

Day Five/8:00 AM: Our disease had so much control over our lives, that it not only made us do things we did not want to do, but would not let us do things that we wanted to.

My disease used to make my choices. Now I do.

Day Five/9:00 AM: The spiritual journey is one of continually falling on your face, getting up, brushing yourself off, looking sheepishly at God, and taking another step.

If I'm faced in the right direction, and fall on my face, I've still made progress.

Day Five/10:00 AM: Whatever you are trying to avoid, we won't go away until you confront it.

When I see myself as others see me, do I deny it?

Day Five/11:00 AM: It's a very interesting thing about human nature, when you stop treating yourself poorly, it will become unacceptable for others to do so.

If I don't take care of myself, why should anyone else?

Day Five/12:00 PM: What you give your attention to governs your life. In active addiction, we give our attention to alcohol and drugs. In early recovery, our attention is governed by "not picking up." Thus "the struggle" against drugs governs our life. It is only when our attention is on "practicing principles" that we can truly claim we are "in recovery."

Whatever I resist, persists.

Day Five/1:00 PM: Pity Pot: Poor me, poor me, pour me a drink.

I profit not from the pity pot, pour me a cup of coffee (at a meeting!).

Day Five/2:00 PM: Do you think you deserve special treatment because you are clean and sober? Most of us do at one time or another. Treat us special and we feel normal; treat us normal and we feel rejected.

Do I want my ego to be the first thing people see when I walk into a room?

Day Five/3:00 PM: Guilt is the reverse side of Arrogance. Guilt aims at self-destruction. Arrogance aims at the destruction of others. Acceptance is the answer.

When I accept that my past is never going to change, guilt and arrogance are rendered neutral.

Day Five/4:00 PM: Even when it hurts like hell, hold fast. The pain is the arrow coming out, not the arrow going in. Faith is not about trusting a God who will rescue you from arrows but trusting in the process. Faith will center you, not rescue you.

As the pain and fear pass, I hold fast.

Day Five/5:00 PM: If people don't agree with you, so what? If people do agree with you, so what? Our program is one of suggestions, not conformity.

I do not need to conform to be comfortable. "Comfortable" is conscious contact, not conscious copycat.

Day Five/6:00 PM: Alcoholism is an equal opportunity destroyer and the Twelve Step program is an equal opportunity restorer. This is about tolerance when we carry the message.

Kindness is in my power even when affection is not.

Day Five/7:00 PM: All of us chemical dependents have come from the same place, *no where.* We all enter the world of recovery by changing our place to *now here. No Where* to *Now Here.* It works.

NOW is the working unit of my life.

Day Five/8:00 PM: There are no victims, only volunteers. When we cry, "They did this to me, they did that to me…" what we are really saying, is I placed myself in a position for this or that to happen. I volunteered for it.

I volunteer for sobriety today.

Day Five/9:00 PM: Day: Have you identified yourself clearly as a chemically dependent person suffering from a chronic disease? We have tricky minds and it is oh, so easy to play games with labels and convince ourselves we can use this chemical and that drug because that is not our main addiction. In this disease, only abstinence paves the way to recovery.

I suffer from chemical dependency, addiction, alcoholism, or whatever I chose to call this disease. I do not use "labels" to allow me to deny that any mood-altering, mind-affecting chemical is poison to me.

Day Five/10:00 PM: Addicts are famous for producing little playlets of what should have been said, when it should have said, how things might have been better or different. They get stuck in reruns of the past and forget that change only occurs in the now.

I don't write scripts unless I'm going to publish them.

Day Five/11:00 PM: He who laughs, lasts! "But why shouldn't we laugh? We have recovered." (P 132, AA Big Book)

My laughter is good medicine.

§

Day Six/12:00 AM: You certainly are not good at *every aspect* of service to your group. You may be good at opening meetings, emptying ash trays, remembering to contact people, or going out on Twelve Step calls. Maybe you are lousy at greeting people at the door, holding office, getting birthday cakes, or paying the rent. Whatever you lack skills for, others can pick up; whatever you are good at, recognize!

For my shortcomings, I delegate; for my strengths, I congratulate.

Day Six/1:00 AM: The steps are to get us well. The traditions are to get the group well. Since we are part of the group, we must also work the traditions.

Not only do I ask, "What step am I on?" to keep fit, I also ask, "Is there a tradition that applies to this?"

Day Six/2:00 AM: "Being angry at God won't hurt God, and neither will it provoke Him to take measures against us. If it makes us feel better to vent our anger at Him over a painful situation, we are free to do it. The only thing wrong with doing it is that what happened to us was not really God's fault." ~Harold S. Kushner, *When Bad Things Happen to Good People*

Usually, things don't happen TO make me angry; things happen THAT make me angry.

Day Six/3:00 AM: Some of the greatest disappointments in life have come from that which we insisted upon having. Working Step Three will save us from the worst of "I got to have it" type disappointments.

I am careful what I pray for; I just may get it!

Day Six/4:00 AM: You can *react* to situations that arise or you can *respond* to them. This is an important distinction. *Reacting* is done instinctively, without thought, while *responding* requires thought and choice.

I delay my reactions so that I can <u>respond</u> to situations that used to baffle me.

Day Six/5:00 AM: Life begins right outside your comfort zone. Start changing.

If I fail to change the person I was when I came in, that person will take me out!

Day Six/6:00 AM: Tomorrow is not a day to worry about. Yes, there are possible adversities, burdens, and fears but the sun will rise without our control and we know not whether it rises in splendor or behind a mask of stormy weather.

I needn't worry about tomorrow, my Higher Power is already there.

Day Six/7:00 AM: If you are not happy with what you have, what makes you think you would be happy with more?

Happiness is not having what I want but wanting what I have.

Day Six/8:00 AM: Others may pity you when you don't want them to and then they won't when you do. Likewise, you will pity yourself at times and then be sick of it. Do the best you can and things will turn out better than you planned.

Things turn out the best when I make the best of the way things turn out.

Day Six/9:00 AM: One way to tell how well you are practicing the principles in all your affairs is to notice how you treat people who can be of no service to you.

I go out of my way to be kind to the very next person I encounter, regardless of what they can or cannot do for me.

Day Six/10:00 AM: It is our experience in recovery that a Power greater then ourselves places the answers before us that we need to hear when we need to hear them. Often we don't like the answers and practice self-will by trying to force *our* solution. Forcing solutions is the same as ignoring Step Three.

When I force the solution, the solution becomes the problem.

Day Six/11:00 AM: Yes, you take them to meetings, but can't make them listen; you give them a basic text but you can't make them read it; you set a good example but you can't stop them from picking up.

I pick them up, as long as they don't pick up.

Day Six/12:00 PM: Whatever spiritual values you adopt are unique to you. You may adopt a strong religious stance or a more intimate spiritual philosophy from within. In any case, the spiritual path you seek is up to you and not those around you. Be comfortable with your spiritual choices and don't try to please others.

The more I have on the inside, the less I need on the outside.

Day Six/1:00 PM: The pessimist sees only the tunnel. The optimist sees the light at the end of the tunnel. The fatalist sees the tunnel, the light at the end and the next tunnel after that!

In recovery, I know that the light at the end of the tunnel is no longer an on-coming train.

Day Six/2:00 PM: Prayer does not change what you are praying about. Prayer changes you.

I learn to "hit" it with a prayer, not a chair and I change!

Day Six/3:00 PM: All our suggestions are free. The ones you don't take are the ones you end up paying for.

When all else fails, I take the suggestions.

Day Six/4:00 PM: There is no magic for getting clean and sober. It is simply putting one sober step in front of the other. You don't want to miss real recovery looking for magic, do you? There is no magic that will make addiction go away. Forget rapid detox, hypnosis, and wishing it away; the meaning and magic are in your principles.

I find the answers, meaning,
and magic in me and my program.

Day Six/5:00 PM: We find that the winners do what they have to do and the losers do what they want to do.

The winners are stuck with me.

Day Six/6:00 PM: There are two times when you need to go to a meeting, when you think you need one and when you know you don't.

Rather than thinking about going to a meeting, I go
to the meeting, and then think about it.

Day Six/7:00 PM: Here is a thought that kills a lot of chemical dependents: That may be true for you, but I'm different. We call it terminal uniqueness.

I celebrate that fact that what I thought made me special
and different are the things I have most in common
with other alcoholics and addicts!

Day Six/8:00 PM: Another short version of Steps One, Two, and Three: Just Accept, Don't Reject, and Don't Expect.

I accept that I am powerless over mind-affecting, mood-
altering chemicals; I don't reject the possibility that God
can do this; I don't expect things to turn out my way

once I've turned it over to God.

Day Six/9:00 PM: Opportunities are often disguised as problems and this is why we miss them. With the next problem you encounter, ask, "What can I learn from this?"

I watch for big problems; they disguise big opportunities.

Day Six/10:00 PM: Alcoholics use the word "confusion" as a smokescreen so they can stay in self-will. The truth is, you are not really confused, most of the time. If you give up your confusion, you can't do what you want, you have to do what is right.

I take the "con" out of confusion, and fuse my will to that of my Higher Power.

Day Six/11:00 PM: They say you need newcomers to tell you where you came from, old-timers to tell you where you could go, and a sponsor to tell you where you are at.

The most important word in my Steps is the first one... "WE"

§

Day Seven/12:00 AM: You may occasionally go over things in your mind ad-nauseam, seemingly unable to control rogue thoughts. Your blood pressure goes up as your mind races over the same details again and again. Then, you can't sleep. But remember what the old timers say, "A lack of sleep never killed anybody!"

When I can't sleep, I don't count sheep,
I talk to the Shepard.

Day Seven/1:00 AM: Grateful addicts don't drink and drug and drinking and drugging addicts aren't grateful.

My gratitude is not the word but my desire to say the word. My desire to say the word is a corner stone of my recovery.

Day Seven/2:00 AM: Is yesterday something that you worry about? Some yesterday? Whatever its mistakes, faults, blunders, or pains it has passed forever beyond your control. Accept that you cannot erase a single word or deed from your "yesterdays."

I regain my sanity when I quit hoping for a better past. Everything is as it should be now.

Day Seven/3:00 AM: "To doubt everything or to believe everything are two equally convenient solutions; both dispense with the necessity of reflection." ~Jules Henri Poincsre

I question myself, "Am I a nay sayer to all suggestions?" or equally destructive "Am I a disciple of a God Squad, blindly following a hard and inflexible line of thought?"

Day Seven/4:00 AM: If you think you can or you think you can't, you're probably right.

The state of my world is a reflection of the state of my mind.

Day Seven/5:00 AM: "It is time to speak your Truth. Create your community. Be good to each other. And do not look outside yourself for the leader. This could be a good time!" *Oraibi, Arizona Hopi Nation*

I enjoy the Fellowship of the Spirit.

Day Seven/6:00 AM: Undoubtedly you lament making so many bad decisions before you found the program. Remember, even Babe Ruth struck out 1383 times. Of course, this disease robbed you of many home runs at a younger age, yet today it offers new plays.

I am no longer striking out, but hitting balls high and far as I practice batting principles and making home (group) runs! <smile>

Day Seven/7:00 AM: When dealing with conflicts inside

the group, it doesn't matter so much who is right, but what is right.

Am I placing principles before my ego?

Day Seven/8:00 AM: Listen to the message, not the messenger! This is what Tradition Twelve is all about, looking past the personality to the principle behind the message. There are some mighty slick personalities out there talking trash and some Big Book thumpers (irritating as they are) that have a true message of hope.

The slicker, the sicker.

Day Seven/9:00 AM: They say you don't have to like your sponsor; they just have to have something you want—like a life. It is your sponsor's job to give you a program to work until you develop a program of your own.

People who sponsor themselves have fools for sponsors.

Day Seven/10:00 AM: When one door closes, another door opens. It's waiting in the hallway that's hell.

I am not a slow learner. I am just, sometimes, a slow accepter.

Day Seven/11:00 AM: Many people think that the Twelve Steps are the work. But they are not. The Twelve Steps are the *preparation* for doing the real work. The real work is in reaching out to the still suffering alcoholic and addict. God has no hands but yours. (attributed to Mother Theresa).

I become the hands of my Higher Power.

Day Seven/12:00 PM: Most of our growth in recovery takes *time*. You may, like many of us, want to be restored to wholeness yesterday. However, you can afford to be patient. After all, when the Universe made time, it made plenty of it.

I give time, time.

Day Seven/1:00 PM: "There is no such thing as chance; and what to us seems merest accident springs from the deepest source of destiny." ~Friedrich von Schiller

Everything happening is in God's plan for me today.

Day Seven/2:00 PM: Do not be quick to call all therapy "psyco-babble" and think that mental health experts do not understand. Therapy can be the guide that leads you to the discovery of your anchor amidst the surrounding storms of life.

In the words of Bill Wilson, I should "never belittle a good doctor or psychiatrist".

Day Seven/3:00 PM: In the words of Wayne Dryer "You will be happy to know that the universal law that created miracles has not been repealed."

I Expect a Miracle today.

Day Seven/4:00 PM: We came here for our drinking and stay here for our thinking.

It was not my best thinking that got me drunk, it was my best drinking. My best thinking got me here.

Day Seven/5:00 PM: We came here for our drugging and stay in part for hugging.

Hugs are one way the fellowship demonstrates to me that it isn't "me" and "you" anymore, it's "we" and "us."

Day Seven/6:00 PM: The soul would have no rainbow if the eyes had no tears. ~Indian Proverb. Our program was born out of trouble and tears, the most serious kinds of trouble and bitterest of tears. That makes our rainbows all the brighter.

My soul is promised rainbows of recovery.

Day Seven/7:00 PM: Yes, there are times you can't

sleep, someone hurts your feelings, the dog pisses on your carpet, and the boss doesn't like your work. Take two aspirin and adjust!

Nothing is going to happen to me
that You and I can't handle together.

Day Seven/8:00 PM: The person you were will use again. That is why you must "smash all your old ideas" so that the *new you* is a member of the program, not the person you were. The person you were was a practicing alcoholic. The person you are is not.

Some people say that the 12 Steps brain wash us.
Thank God, because that's how I got clean!

Day Seven/9:00 PM: Yesterday is but a dream, tomorrow but a vision. Today well lived is a gift, that's why they call it the "Present."

Going to bed tonight clean and sober,
is my present to myself!

Day Seven/10:00 PM: The best remedy for anger is delay.

I don't use my "claws when agitated," I learn to
"pause when agitated." (P 87, AA Big Book)

Day Seven/11:00 PM: "Opened by mistake" applies to the mouth more often than it does to mail. In order not to become one of those "personalities" that people are trying to put principles before—learn to pause and ask for guidance before speaking.

I learn to hold my tongue until it has consulted my soul.

WEEK TWO

Day Eight/12:00 AM: Some people quote the Bible, Qur'an, Torah, or some other holy text claiming that it is your only road to recovery. You may or may not find that comforting. Whether or not it is comforting you, remember it is comforting them. Be tolerant and gracious.

I may not find something personally helpful,
but I find it helpful to be personable.

Day Eight/1:00 AM: When things go wrong, they are not particularly anyone's fault. You can't expect every meeting to be perfect and your sponsor to have every answer. You know you can't control or fix everything that goes wrong and neither can "they."

When things go wrong, I don't let them get too far.

Day Eight/2:00 AM: KISS. Keep It Simple Stupid. We are not suggesting we are stupid, but *our disease is.* It will do anything it can to keep us using even though it ultimately means the death of itself along with the body. But through following a few SIMPLE suggestions, we can extract ourselves from the stupidity.

My stupid disease will argue and complicate even
the simplest of understandings. I tell my
addictive thinking to kiss off!

Day Eight/3:00 AM: When you come down off the pink cloud of new found recovery, it is all to easy to walk with your head in the clouds of new found spirituality. You can't see where you're going with your head in the clouds!

I do not become so spiritual that I am of no earthly value.

Day Eight/4:00 AM: Fragments of our addiction never stop calling, "Hey, just one won't hurt; look, what's so wrong with going to that party; it's disloyal to stop seeing old friends." But those of us who've been around awhile recognize the "callings" for what they are. Give the "calls" an inch and we KNOW addiction takes a mile.

I hope for the best, but prepare for the thirst.

Day Eight/5:00 AM: The diversity of people seeking recovery is extraordinary. Whether an old salty dog, young gang member, grandparent, or teen with attitude, we remember: as cancer is no respecter of victims, neither is addiction. Same disease, same recovery.

"We all came on different ships, but we're all on the same boat now." ~Martin Luther King

Day Eight/6:00 AM: How is your spiritual condition this morning? Does it need reconditioning? The gift of recovery is contingent upon the replenishment of our spiritual program *every single day*. What goes into your spiritual reconditioning this morning?

My reprieve from using is a daily grace contingent upon my spiritual base.

Day Eight/7:00 AM: "Without freedom from the past there is no freedom at all, because the mind is never new, fresh, innocent. It is only the fresh, innocent mind that is free." ~J. Krishnamurti, *The Book of Life*

I Uncover...Discover...Discard, making my mind new, fresh, and innocent.

Day Eight/8:00 AM: In our fellowship, there are always those who feel they have the ultimate wisdom to impart to you. These highly verbose people may set your nerves on edge with incredibly self-serving "words of wisdom." They may be full of themselves, but they are probably not trying to hurt you.

If I judge people, I have no time to love them.

Day Eight/9:00 AM: People, places, and things are transitory, flitting through our lives at different speeds. We can trust no person, no place, and often not even our own best intentions. We can only trust our spiritual foundation.

Turning my will and life over to a Power greater than myself is the ultimate in trust. Did I greet this day with the Third Step?

Day Eight/10:00 AM: Today, don't get caught up with what's wrong with your job. Today you have a job. Today, don't get caught up with what's wrong with your car. Today you have one. Don't get caught up with what's wrong with you life, today you have a life.

Just for today...

Day Eight/11:00 AM: In order to grasp recovery we must learn, not accumulate knowledge, but really learn. Accumulating knowledge is moving from the known to the known, but *learning* is moving from the known to the unknown.

Each time I say, "Thy will, not mine, be done," I move from the known to the unknown and I can learn.

Day Eight/12:00 PM: "People are always blaming their circumstances for being what they are. The people who get on in this world are the people who get up and look for the circumstances they want, and if they can't find them, make them." ~George Bernard Shaw

As long as I blame my past, I'm not free to claim my future.

Day Eight/1:00 PM: People will tell you to "work" the steps and that may lead you to believe that the steps are our work in recovery. Working the steps is not doing our work, they are the foundation for doing our work. Our work is getting into the trenches and helping others.

When my life is not working the way I want it to,
I find I may not be doing my real work.

Day Eight/2:00 PM: They say that if you want to make God laugh, just tell Her/Him your plans for the day.

I plan plans, not results.

Day Eight/3:00 PM: One of the joys of this program is the path it provides us with to do the right thing. Our steps don't give us a whole lot of room for justifications. There is no right way to do the wrong thing.

I learn to do the next right thing, not the next "me" thing.

Day Eight/4:00 PM: Forgive yourself because your Spiritual Source already has. Who are you to argue about this?

T.G.I.F.: Thank God I'm Forgiven.

Day Eight/5:00 PM: Sobriety is a grant, not a gift. A gift is something we get to keep forever. A grant is contingent on us doing something to keep it.

I work steps because my recovery is "contingent on the maintenance of {my} spiritual program."
(P 85, AA Book)

Day Eight/6:00 PM: You can not right all your past. In our program, you learn to clear away what wreckage you can and then you have to let it go. This is why you must "Let God do for you what you can not do for yourself."

When I question my Higher Power on what can be done about this, HP already has me working on the problem.

Day Eight/7:00 PM: You may be falling apart, you may be "being strong," or you may be falling apart and trying very hard to "be strong." No matter what you are doing, someone will be telling you that you "should" respond differently. So respond how you respond in your recovery. Just don't pick up!

I respond the way I respond and it must be right, because I'm clean and sober now!

Day Eight/8:00 PM: "You can't laugh and think at the same time! So every time you laugh you're getting a break from you." ~Ken D. (P 153, *Alkiespeak*)

I take my program seriously, not myself.

Day Eight/9:00 PM: God helps those who let Him do His job.

There is only one thing I need to know about God; it's not me!

Day Eight/10:00 PM: Although a bit of compassion might be nice now and again, you sure don't need anyone's pity! Compassion is laced with understanding while pity reflects a diminished picture of yourself. With gut level honesty, you will evoke compassion; by denying, hiding, and blaming, you are likely to evoke pity from others.

If I am genuine about my recovery with others, they will be genuine in their compassion with me.

Day Eight/11:00 PM: Although romance and relationships are an important aspect of balance in our lives--it is never the solution to drinking and other drug taking. It is sometimes easier to focus on passion, rather than trudge through the steps!

I practice these principles in all my affairs, (pun intended).

§

Day Nine/12:00 AM: Everyday in our lives is not going to be perfect just because we are not drinking or drugging. The best way we know of to treat PMS (Poor Me Syndrome) is get rid of the words "It ain't fair" and "Why me?"

God does ot owe me happiness because I no longer am an intolerant, abusive, self-centered, practicing addict.

Day Nine/1:00 AM: You must learn to pick up a program, not just set down a drink! They call this foot work. Your Higher Power wants to make a deal with you. You do the foot work and He'll take care of the results.

If I have one hand in the fellowship and one hand in God's, I can't pick up today.

Day Nine/2:00 AM: There is a simple 20/20 plan so you can *see* how our program works. Come to the meetings 20 minutes before they start, stay 20 minutes after they are over and *see* what happens.

I "carry the vision of God's will into all {my} activities." (P 85, AA Big Book)

Day Nine/3:00 AM: There will be many times when nothing anyone does, including yourself, seems right. But these "nothing is ever right" times pass like a cloud overhead. Do not make decisions until the cloud passes, so that you make them in the full light of your good senses.

I do not make decisions when "nothing is going right." How can my decision be right if nothing else is?

Day Nine/4:00 AM: Your low feelings will always pass. Your high feelings will also pass. The tide comes in, the tide goes out. A fact of life. Whatever is high tide in your emotion now, will eventually ebb to low tide.

Nothing is forever.

Day Nine/5:00 AM: No matter what anyone says, change does not have to be a painful process. What is painful is the *resistance to change*. Think. If you never change your socks and shoes, holes will wear in them, you'll get blisters, your feet will smell and it will be painful.

Changing my socks and shoes and changing my attitude

and behavior are the same--it keeps me fresh, clean, and able to take Steps, painlessly.

Day Nine/6:00 AM: It is not unusual for people to say something and then consider it done. They forget to actually do it. Do not say "I will go to more meetings; I will get a sponsor soon; I must work with newcomers," then consider it done. You must actually do these things to have them work for you.

I let go of doing life in my head.

Day Nine/7:00 AM: "We can reach UP for that energy, and we can reach IN for that energy, feel that life force, touch that *Power Greater Than Ourselves.* We can reach up and in and hold on and hang in there. If we just stop... We can climb up from that dark hole. And be here. Be present. Be awake for the next miracle." ~Ruth Fishel, *Hang in 'Til the Miracle Happens*

I reach up and in, hold on and hang in.

Day Nine/8:00 AM: Don't allow anger, bitterness, and other character defects to affect your family, friends, and fellowship. It is all too easy to lash out at ones close to you who will "understand" your hostility and give you room because you are in recovery. Treat them as you would a newcomer for they deserve as much.

Harsh words break no bones but they do break hearts.

Day Nine/9:00 AM: This is a "We" program, not a "Me" program. We do this together. Look at our steps. They all say "We admitted" or "We came to believe..." Doing it together makes us stronger and less likely to fool ourselves with dysfunctional ways of thinking.

This is a self-help program that I can't do by myself.

Day Nine/10:00 AM: Our society usually stresses that pain and sadness are to be avoided at all costs. If you hurt longer then five minutes, they imply, it's a symptom of neurosis. Yet pain and sadness is what you are designed to feel during tough times. It's a healthy reaction, not an "unwell" one. Don't be unhappy about being unhappy.

I live with only one unhappiness at a time. I choose not to be unhappy about being unhappy.

Day Nine/11:00 AM: HALT. Don't get too Hungry, too Angry, too Lonely, too Tired. You already know this, yet how often do you overlook it? Don't let addiction suck you into using some mind-affecting chemical simply because you brushed aside such a "simple" suggestion. The longer you are clean and sober, the easier it is to brush "simple" suggestions aside.

Most great points in our program are simple. I eat when hungry, call my sponsor when angry, find a meeting when lonely, rest when tired.

Day Nine/12:00 PM: Any of us can use our concept of God to rant and rave at, to vent frustrations. If you believe in a Higher Power or you don't, it doesn't matter. If you rant at god and there is none, no harm done. IF you rant at god and God exists, no harm done. A loving God understands and absorbs your pain.

I vent my frustrations toward a Universal Intelligence, not others who may be unable and unwilling to absorb my pain.

Day Nine/1:00 PM: Seven days without a meeting, makes one weak.

Just as I am not independently wealthy and need to work to stay solvent, I am not independently healthy and need meetings to stay soulvent.

Day Nine/2:00 PM: "Smile facts: It is 2.5 times easier to smile than to frown. It takes 43 muscles to frown, but only 17 to smile. Smiling stimulates our nervous system to produce 'cerebral morphine.' This hormone give us a pleasant feeling and it has an anesthetic effect." ~Karlynn Baker Scharlau, *A Thoughtful Moment*

When I meet someone today who isn't wearing a smile,
I give them mine.

Day Nine/3:00 PM: Recovery is not the absence of conflict but the ability to cope with it.

My recovery comes from new daily habits I form in seconds, minutes, and hours of simple Twelve-Step living.

Day Nine/4:00 PM: Get a sponsor; get a program; get into service; get a Higher Power in your life; get a life; get it right. Wake up and smell the recovery.

When I am tempted to think these clean and sober people are full of shit, let me remember that they're full of clean and sober shit.

Day Nine/5:00 PM: Sobriety often brings us effects we never expected, like becoming the person we used to resent!

I used to resent people whose standards I could not live up to. Now, by the Grace of God, I am one!

Day Nine/6:00 PM: There are people in the program who will tell you that you mustn't be exposed to drugs or alcohol at all or that you will slip. Our experience shows that this is not necessarily so. "We must meet these conditions every day," it says in the AA Big Book. An alcoholic and addict who cannot meet them still has an alcoholic/addict mind. Your only chance for sobriety would be to be locked up and even then other inmates would have drugs and alcohol.

Every where I go, there I am! Thus it is my spiritual foundation that keeps me safe, not "exposure" or lack thereof to the real world.

Day Nine/7:00 PM: Being lonely gets in the way of

learning how to live alone. You are not alone even though you may have felt alone in a crowd in the past. The remedy for loneliness is service. Show up to a meeting 30 minutes early tonight and help set up. We promise you will not be lonely!

I never have to be alone again.

Day Nine/8:00 PM: Having a God of our own understanding does not mean we have to withhold saying "God" around non-believers. People who try to get the word "God" out of the Twelve Steps in order not to offend others, are missing the point. The point is, no one *has* to say "God" in order to recover—it does not mean others can't call their Higher Power "God."

God is the answer. Now what is my problem?

Day Nine/9:00 PM: Have you ever found yourself saying, "*I can't believe this*!" because things have gotten out of hand? You can't believe it because it's gotten out of *your* hand. This is the time to laugh at yourself for trying to control again—poke fun at the situation, your beliefs, whatever. Have fun.

"When things get goofy beyond belief, it's time to stop believing and get goofy." ~Pat Samples, Daily Comforts for Caregivers

Day Nine/10:00 PM: Crying can be very soothing. Yet tears don't always come when you want them to. Maybe messages from the past like "Big boys don't cry" or "Don't be a cry-baby," stop the soothing tears you need to express. Begin to reverse these messages so your subconscious can release you, "Big boys do cry" and "Crying is healthy for babies *and* adults."

My subconscious is my friend when I give it the right messages. Big boys and girls do cry and tears are healthy for adults and babies alike.

Day Nine/11:00 PM: We always wanted our image to be good, yet we always seemed to come off bad. Chemicals just made us think we were OK, but it was an illusion that quickly fell apart every morning. Chemicals built an illusion but character, based on principle, builds the true image we seek.

I now wake up with my Character, not the aftermath of chemicals, and I no longer worry about the morning after!

§

Day Ten/12:00 AM: Occasionally, seizing a HALT moment, the Babbler begins a silent running dialogue in your head ready to put you down because you are vulnerable, "You're stupid; they're stupid; who wants sobriety; boy, is this dumb." Babbler is not the voice of your Higher Power. It is the voice of addiction capitalizing on a HALT moment.

My Higher Power does not put me down. When the Babbler begins, I call a HALT to it by taking care of myself.

Day Ten/1:00 AM: It is not your duty to solve other people's problems, arbitrate their disputes and raise their children. If you believe this is Twelve Step work, you will only be hurt when they reject your advice and shocked when they blame you for their troubles.

My job is to carry the message, not deliver the drunk.

Day Ten/2:00 AM: If you don't stand for something, they say you will fall for anything. Do you stand up for recovery? Do you stand up for principle? Do you stand up for the Traditions, Steps, and Fellowship?

United we stand; divided we stagger.

Day Ten/3:00 AM: Although thoughts are things, they are not actions; although feelings are real, they are not facts. They only have the power we give them through our actions.

When I act kindly, I give power to loving thoughts and feelings; when I use harsh words and "get even" I give power to angry thoughts and feelings.

Day Ten/4:00 AM: They say that young people don't get sober, they get caught. Getting caught is a great way to find recovery. We don't care how you get here, whether it is your parents that force you, a school counselor, the courts, or a guilty conscious--you're here. So decide not to get recaught, but to recover instead.

If I'm young, I am respectful of the old farts. If I'm an old fart I don't recite platitudes to the young.

Day Ten/5:00 AM: Although there are no Twelve Step gurus, and God knows we are not saints, there are times when the words and actions of some members touch us so much that we practically consider them saints. We never forget though, that they are human and still suffer. So we reach out to them as they reach out to others.

I remember that the "alcoholic that still suffers" could just as well be an old-timer as it is a newcomer, my sponsor as my sponsee.

Day Ten/6:00 AM: "Suit up, Show up, Sit up, Shut up" is what we used to tell newcomers. We used to say this for darn good reason. Drunk drunks and newly clean addicts shouldn't be running at the mouth about recovery when they don't understand recovery. Unfortunately "Politically Correct" (or rather, "Therapeutically Correct") often hijacks our meetings. Do not be afraid to take our meetings back.

In order to continue to help the newcomer, I Suit up, Show up, Sit up, and Speak up!

Day Ten/7:00 AM: The old timers used to say that the

world's most difficult prayer was "O, Lord, be as good to me today, as I was to my fellowman, yesterday."

I say what I mean, mean what I say,
and don't say it mean.

Day Ten/8:00 AM: If God is your co-pilot, switch seats! (Anonymous Sage) There is something special waiting for you to do today that won't get done if you are flying around doing your own thing.

When I let my Higher Power pilot my life, I know that
inspiration will guide my actions and that
"special something" will get done.

Day Ten/9:00 AM: Right now, whatever is bothering you, set it aside. Turn to the next person you see and smile. Tell them "hi" and wish them well. This is the First Step to getting out of self.

As I reach out to let another know how valuable they are,
I immediately set the stage to become part of the
answer and not part of the problem.

Day Ten/10:00 AM: Don't ever think you have nothing left to learn in the fellowship and that everyone wants to hear you talk incessantly because you are so wise. You can not have an open mouth and an open mind at the same time.

When I do all the talking, I can only
hear what I already know.

Day Ten/11:00 AM: We are now learning to keep our thoughts in recovery and not in the insanity of the past. The program fixes it so we don't have to suffer from insanity anymore. Now we can enjoy it!

Crazy-making is what I make of it.

Day Ten/12:00 PM: Few of us realize that God is all we need until God is all we have.

If I can't find God, I know who moved.

Day Ten/1:00 PM: Our incessant analyzing could very well lead us to some pretty stupid behavior. Is your mind yapping at you constantly? "I don't need a meeting; sponsoring myself is fine; I could use a sleeping aid, after all I only drank." When your goals are clear, so is your mind.

I change my behavior to meet my goals,
not my goals to meet my behavior.

Day Ten/2:00 PM: If you rely on meetings alone to keep you sober, then you must find a 24 hour meeting. Meetings are for identifying and sharing. People in the meetings will tell you what they did and suggest what you can do, but they can't do it for you.

I can pray for a good harvest, but I still have to plow.

Day Ten/3:00 PM: Don't let your starting point in recovery ever discourage you. Don't let your starting point today put a frown on your face. Anyone who gets to be an old-timer had to be a newcomer first. Smile and start.

My journey of a thousand smiles
begins with the First Step.

Day Ten/4:00 PM: It seems insane that we have to be brought to our knees before we seek help, but for most of us that's the way it is. Few of us seek the discomfort of growth and change until what we are doing makes us so darn *uncomfortable* that we can't stand it anymore.

When my comfort zone is no longer comfortable,
I comfort myself knowing that I am about to grow.

Day Ten/5:00 PM: "When one is a stranger to oneself then one is estranged from others too. If one is out of touch with oneself, then one cannot touch others." ~Anne Morrow Lindbergh, *Gifts From the Sea* 1955

I cannot touch others if I am not in touch with myself. I keep in touch with myself through Step Ten.

Day Ten/6:00 PM: We are not exempt from the crap in life because we are sober. The universe does not give us special dispensation because we work the Twelve Steps. However, we remember that today we have more solutions than problems.

I make the solution so big, the crap does not exist.

Day Ten/7:00 PM: The most convincing message we can carry to other chemical dependents is our own example of a contented recovery. And kindness. To the desolate alcoholic/addict, an act of kindness can be the difference between getting "better" or getting "bitter."

I remember that I may be the only
Big Book some people ever see.

Day Ten/8:00 PM: Did you *actually* listen to the last person that tried to help you? Your sponsor, counselor, or other group member? Or did you blow off their words because you've heard it all before? If you *listen* with intent to the next person who offers words of support, HP has a message for you.

When I talk, I can only say something I already know.
When I listen, I may learn something
somebody else knows.

Day Ten/9:00 PM: If you don't deal with your feelings, they'll deal with you. Whatever you are thinking right now is creating how you feel. One of the best ways to deal with the way you feel is to create positive thoughts.

I create positive feelings by thinking positive thoughts.

Day Ten/10:00 PM: Knowing what to do with this moment, is as simple as doing the next right thing so that your Spiritual Source can act in your best interests.

When my Higher Power is for me,
what can be against me?

Day Ten/11:00 PM: Now and then with a little time, we stop working one through nine. The price of recovery is eternal vigilance. Steps Ten, Eleven, and Twelve insure that we keep working One through Nine.

No matter how much time I have from my last drink or drug, I am only Twelve Steps away from the next.

§

Day Eleven/12:00 AM: Whatever our problems, when we dwell on the problem, the problem gets bigger. When we dwell on the solution, the solution gets bigger.

I don't tell my Higher Power how big my problem is,
I tell my problem how big my Higher Power is.

Day Eleven/1:00 AM: Our recovery has less to do with our thinking and much more to do with our actions. If you don't believe this, stop going to meetings, stop looking at where you're wrong, stop making amends, and stop doing service work. You will soon see that no matter how good your "thoughts" are, your life won't be worth a hoot in very short order.

My recovery works better when I utilize, not analyze.

Day Eleven/2:00 AM: The next time a newcomer tells you, "The program isn't working for me," agree with them. They are right. Then explain to them that the only people who stay clean and sober are the ones who work the program, not the ones who wait for the program to work for them.

I must do the work or it doesn't get done.

Day Eleven/3:00 AM: "You simply will not be the same person two months from now after consciously giving thanks each day for the abundance that exists in your life. And you will have set in motion an ancient spiritual law:

the more you have and are grateful for, the more will be given you." ~Sarah Ban Breathnach

Gratitude, that's my attitude.

Day Eleven/4:00 AM: "If you are humble, nothing can touch you, neither praise nor disgrace, because you know who you are." ~Mother Theresa

Humility is that virtue which reduces me to the proper size without degrading me, and increases me in statue without inflating me.

Day Eleven/5:00 AM: Frequently, addicts and alcoholics who experience difficulties will isolate in order to lick their wounds like an injured animal. You may not want to bother us, you may be embarrassed by your blunders, or you may think it's not our business. When you don't use our friendship, we can't do our job.

Friends are God's way of taking care of me.

Day Eleven/6:00 AM: Your recovery comes from the new daily habits you form in seconds, minutes, and hours of simple Twelve-Step living. You can't have tomorrow's growth today, but today's habits create the foundation for tomorrow's growth.

I can't speed up my recovery, but I can sure slow it down!

Day Eleven/7:00 AM: God is the answer, now what is the problem? Problem with the word "God?" According to Random House Dictionary--Life, Truth, Love, Mind, Soul, Spirit, and Principle are all synonymous for "God." The above statement could just as easily be "Life, Truth, Love, Mind, Soul, Spirit, and Principle are the answers. Now what is the problem?"

Today, I let go of the labels that stand between me and my understanding of God.

Day Eleven/8:00 AM: There will be times when people

around you act like absolute jerks. If they are a jerk and the problem is with them, time will reveal it. Likewise, if you are the jerk and the problem is with you, time will reveal it. Do the next right thing and give time time.

Today, I don't let assholes rent space in my head.

Day Eleven/9:00 AM: You may not always know what is right but you sure know what is wrong. Anytime you have to give *excuses* for why you do what you do, it's wrong.

If I have to explain or excuse it, then I can do without it.

Day Eleven/10:00 AM: One thing recovery teaches us, is that you *can* keep going long after you think you can't. This is because you are stronger than you think. You have the accumulated strength of millions of clean and sober Twelve-Step members to bolster you.

I keep on keep'n on; I keep on trudging.

Day Eleven/11:00 AM: Relief Lies in Two Four Letter Words that Begin with *F*: Steps Four and Five. (P 29, *Young, Sober, & Free*)

I Uncover to Recover in Four and Five.

Day Eleven/12:00 PM: Be careful of your thoughts--they may become your actions. Be careful of your actions--they may become your habits. Be careful of your habits--they may become your character. Be careful of your character--it reflects your recovery (or lack thereof).

My thoughts are like food for my soul.
I am careful what I feed it.

Day Eleven/1:00 PM: Learn from the mistakes of others. You can't live long enough to make them all yourself.

My sponsor's mistakes become my gifts when I listen.

Day Eleven/2:00 PM: "Living life on life's terms," just what does this mean to us? It *doesn't* mean we will get a brownie button for every day we stay abstinent. It simply means life can be tough *and* we can stay sober if we chose to live by principle.

"Don't you worry none, just take it like it comes, one day at a time." Song, One Day at a Time

Day Eleven/3:00 PM: This is a "We" program, not a "Me" program. We do this together. Look at our steps. They all say "We admitted" or "We came to believe..." Doing it together makes us stronger and less likely to fool ourselves with dysfunctional ways of thinking.

Recovery, it's a WE thing.

Day Eleven/4:00 PM: To err is human but you need to admit it.

I accept that having all the answers is not the answer.

Day Eleven/5:00 PM: Although loving and being loved is an important aspect of balance in our lives—relationships are never the solution to drinking and other drug taking. We sometimes focus on the strong emotion of love from another rather than face loving ourselves by working the program.

Today I "act as if" I am worth loving.

Day Eleven/6:00 PM: When you hear the same platitudes meeting *after meeting*, it can seem like a dog chewing a bone. There seems to be nothing there, yet they keep gnawing away. Actually, it's very useful for the dog to gnaw on the bone (to strengthen teeth and gums) and it is helpful for you to gnaw on the repetitions in the meetings (to strengthen the message).

From repetition comes recognition, as I gnaw on words of recovery.

Day Eleven/7:00 PM: It's not your Higher Power's Will that makes you miserable. It's your *resistance* to HP's

Will that causes the damage. Turning it over will set you right again.

God's will is when I turn it over.
Self-will is when I've over turned it.

Day Eleven/8:00 PM: If you meet more than three assholes in one day, you need a meeting. If you meet more than four, you need a meeting *and to call your sponsor*. Any more than that and you better be reviewing Steps One, Two and Three real hard.

When too many assholes get in my way, it means
I need a check-up from the neck up.

Day Eleven/9:00 PM: What comes after ninety days? Ninety-one! "Even if you're on the right track, you'll get run over if you just sit there." ~Will Rogers

There are only two times I have to diligently work this
program, the first 90 days and every day after that!

Day Eleven/10:00 PM: Rather than getting even with those that hurt you, the challenge is to get even with those that help you.

I can't be resentful and grateful at the same time.

Day Eleven/11:00 PM: Humility is not so much thinking less of yourself as it is thinking of yourself less.

True humility is accepting myself without embellishment
and without embarrassment.

§

Day Twelve/12:00 AM: Don't get 'seeking serenity' confused with 'seeking utopia.' The Twelve-Step programs do not open the gates of heaven to let us in, they open the gates of hell to let us out.

I feel lighter and better about myself when I don't expect
a perfect world simply because I am clean and sober.

Day Twelve/1:00 AM: You must be prepared to make

some unpopular decisions when you live by principle. You will not be able to please everyone. Be firm with others as you chose the principle and not the personality; be firm with your personality as it butts heads with your principles.

By practicing principles in all my affairs, I learn not to "people please" but to "Higher Power Please."

Day Twelve/2:00 AM: Irrational actions and comments made in stress-filled moments can keep you awake at night. If you have said or done something unkind or irrational yesterday, you can resolve the situation by making amends first thing in the morning.

Every minute I am angry with someone, I lose 60 seconds of happiness that I can never get back.

Day Twelve/3:00 AM: We need special people in our lives so that we can travel the path of recovery. The special people are easy to find, they are right in front of you. They are called "winners."

I stick with the winners and win with the stickers.

Day Twelve/4:00 AM: Some people's missionary zeal in helping us is quite annoying. They tell us what to do, know what's best for us, and can get down-right preachy. We, however, can be charitable because we know: they preach best what THEY most need to learn!

My Spiritual Source helps me tolerate the "preachers" of the program; in this way, I contribute to what they need to learn!

Day Twelve/5:00 AM: Progress, not perfection… No matter how long you have been in recovery, no matter how long you have worked the steps, you will never raise above the level of human being.

I claim spiritual progress today, not spiritual perfection.

Day Twelve/6:00 AM: "They say that life is a highway and its milestones are the years, And now and then there's a toll-gate where you buy your way with tears." ~Joyce

There will come a time when I believe everything has ended. That will be the beginning.

Day Twelve/7:00 AM: Many people in meetings speak of remarkable spiritual awakenings in recovery. These awakenings come in many forms; some in a flash of lightening and some in slow revelations. What we know for sure is that they come as a *result of working the steps*, not as a result of wishful thinking.

I woke up this morning clean and sober.
That's my spiritual awakening.

Day Twelve/8:00 AM: People in our fellowships who think they are too big to do little things are perhaps too little to be asked to do big things.

I remember where I came from.

Day Twelve/9:00 AM: Many problems will be averted with a very simple code for behavior. This is called "kindness." Kindness is more then politeness; it means a warm concern for the other person's feelings.

I let my kindness be a gift to another and the tag reads, "Please handle with tender loving care."

Day Twelve/10:00 AM: It is more important to be sober today, than it is to be sober for a long time. Some of us have too many years of recovery and not enough sobriety today.

Today is the most important day of my sobriety.

Day Twelve/11:00 AM: When working with others don't think you haven't got what it takes. If you have *one more day* without a drink or a drug, then you have that one more day to give away.

I can't give away what I don't have, but even one more day sober is worth sharing.

Day Twelve/12:00 PM: "Take the cotton out of your ears and put it in your mouth" applies to the old-timer as well as the beginner—anyone who is too fond of their own voice.

I listen to learn and learn to listen.

Day Twelve/1:00 PM: If there is someone weaker than you, be kind to them. If there is someone stronger than you, be kind to yourself.

What kind of person am I? The kind, kind.

Day Twelve/2:00 PM: Today we have a *choice!* Don't take this gift lightly. You can chose to do right, you can choose to do wrong; with enough wrong choosing, your choices will be gone.

My Higher Power gives the best to me when I give my choice to Him.

Day Twelve/3:00 PM: You don't have to eat, breathe, and bathe in our fellowship, but you *do need* to eat, breathe, and bathe in program. This is because you must practice these principles in all your affairs. The only way to do it in all your affairs is to DO IT in all your affairs.

If I'm working my program, I needn't worry about others working theirs.

Day Twelve/4:00 PM: This too shall pass. Sometimes it passes like a gentle breeze and sometimes it passes kinda like a kidney stone. Whichever, we can *promise* that whatever vexes you now, shall pass.

I give time, time because I know that when God made time, He/She made plenty of it.

Day Twelve/5:00 PM: In the ups and downs of life, remember that the most productive ups and downs are getting up for a meeting and down to the steps.

When I'm down, I take a Step and then the Step takes me.

Day Twelve/6:00 PM: There are many times when crying is the appropriate thing to do. Tears let us know that you need to be supported and consoled. Do not be afraid to cry. Do not be afraid to support others when they cry.

Tears are liquid prayers.

Day Twelve/7:00 PM: You will take a tremendous step toward emotional freedom when you realize you have forgiven your addiction for leaving you. Choose to forgive but never forget, your old sick friend.

It's alcoholism, not alcoholwasm so I can forgive my old sick friend, but not forget.

Day Twelve/8:00 PM: There will always be people who did worse than you and always people who do better. You can use comparison to prove anything you want: that you lack thus and such or that you are better than so and so. We learn not to compare our selves and our stories, but to identify.

I identify, I don't compare.

Day Twelve/9:00 PM: Take heart. There is no situation too difficult to be bettered and no unhappiness too great to be lessened. This is because the spiritual tools you require reside within—within that heart you "take."

What lies in front of me and what lies behind me is insignificant compared to what lies within me.

Day Twelve/10:00 PM: You may sometimes feel like fate made a fool of you with this disease. Why you? This is a normal reaction to any chronic disease just like diabetes, lupus, or others. *We are the fortunate ones* because we can arrest this disease with a simple behavior change, many others can't.

Tonight, I celebrate me.

Day Twelve/11:00 PM: Ramana Marhrshi talks about life's journey and likens it to a train trip. He says that you can carry your baggage on your head or set it on the floor beside you. Either way, both you and your baggage arrive at your destination. This is because the train carries your baggage, not you. If you prefer to carry your burdens on your head, it doesn't change the destination, it simply gives you a head ache.

I chose to let my Higher Power carry my baggage and my burdens.

§

Day Thirteen/12:00 AM: Trying to pray is praying, even when we aren't sure exactly what God wants from us. Trying means we have the *desire* to communicate with the Divine Source. Even if no words come, just hitting your knees means a prayer has occurred.

My healing begins in kneeling.

Day Thirteen/1:00 AM: There is a difference between sharing our experience and imposing our opinions on someone. A sure way to set yourself up for a "slip" is to be convinced that others will slip if they don't listen to your opinion.

When my opinion means more to me than my sobriety, I set myself up for a SLIP (Sobriety Loses Its Priority).

Day Thirteen/2:00 AM: Almost all anger is some form of control—either you trying to control people, places, or things or them trying to control you. If it's you controlling them, stop it. If it's them controlling you, stop it.

I can't do HP's will, my way.

Day Thirteen/3:00 AM: There may be some people who

want you to be perfect. But thanks to our fellowship, to God, and the Twelve Steps, you don't have to be one of them!

I claim progress, not perfection.

Day Thirteen/4:00 AM: Your moods, your attitudes, and thoughts sometimes unfold in ways that baffle you. The "intuition" for dealing with the situations that baffle you is not instantaneous. Unexpectedly, confusion may be lifted for greater understanding, then just as quickly, you may feel baffled once again. Don't make decisions when baffled.

When in doubt, I leave it out.

Day Thirteen/5:00 AM: Our program does not teach us how to handle drinking and drugging. It teaches us how to handle recovery.

Another day, another recovery!

Day Thirteen/6:00 AM: Your awareness of what *could* happen to you in the future may be sharper today than it used to be. However, that doesn't mean that you can see into your future. Thus, each moment you spend planning *results* is probably wasted. However, if you don't *plan* to do the footwork, nothing constructive can move forward in your life.

If I fail to plan, I plan to fail.

Day Thirteen/7:00 AM: If faith without works is dead, then willingness without action is fantasy. You can not say "I'm willing to be honest" and lie, "willing to be open" and ask someone "not to tell" or "willing to have character defects removed" and then beat someone up.

I show genuine willingness through
good actions and not good acting.

Day Thirteen/8:00 AM: It really is a daily program.

Think about it, if you only quit one day at a time, every day that you don't pick up will be an accomplishment. If you quit forever, you won't have accomplished anything until you're dead.

Today, my one day.

Day Thirteen/9:00 AM: Our Twelve-Step program is a program that comforts the disturbed and disturbs the comfortable. It never pays for us to get too comfortable and "rest on our laurels. We are headed for trouble if we do, for alcohol is a subtle foe." (P 85, AA Big Book)

I never did anything in moderation and I'm not about to start with my Steps.

Day Thirteen/10:00 AM: The anguish of addiction will occasionally blindside you, renewing feelings of this seeming injustice—what you lost through your addiction, the ones you hurt, and what might have been. Once you allow for an unjust, impartial world to simply *exist*, you free your spirit to move forward.

What is, is.

Day Thirteen/11:00 AM: Are you afraid of your own anguish? Maybe it's too deep, too frightening? So you avoid expressing it for fear it will take off with your sanity? All growth is not painful but all pain can be growthful. The choice is yours.

I let the anguish gently break my heart and the fellowship gently mend it again, so that my pain becomes a platform for growth.

Day Thirteen/12:00 PM: Safety is not something freely granted by the world. More people are hungry, homeless, sick, and in violent situations, than we care to admit. There are more lives ruined by chemical dependency that we care to admit. Yet the impermanence and insecurity of the earth plane is matched equally with the permanence and safety of the Divine Realm.

My Higher Power gave me a kit of spiritual tools;
I use them to build a durable shelter.

Day Thirteen/1:00 PM: People often protest when they don't get their prayers answered as if the Divine Source is not listening. What they fail to understand is that prayer is not intended to change the situation you are praying about; it is intended to change you.

Life is fragile; I "Handle with Prayer."

Day Thirteen/2:00 PM: Don't ever think you have it made. Your time away from your last mind-affecting chemical is not the same as your distance to the next. You are only one drink away from a drunk, one hit away from a high.

Being sober doesn't keep me sober.

Day Thirteen/3:00 PM: As you work to solve different dilemmas that arise in your life, don't stay so focused on your troubles that you miss discovering the solutions. Give your attention to your Spiritual Source in prayer, meditation, or service to others. By taking your focus off the situation, *soulutions* have a way of finding you.

Through conscious contact, I allow soulutions to find me.

Day Thirteen/4:00 PM: "It works," is the shortest sentence in the AA Big Book and pretty much sums up what the book can do for you. But there's a catch. Keep in mind, the program does not work. *The program does not work*. Just like alcohol doesn't get you drunk. You have to *drink* alcohol in order to get drunk. You have to *work* the program in order for it to work.

It works if I work it.

Day Thirteen/5:00 PM: One hour at a time leads to one day at a time in our recovery. Each hour is one of 24 building blocks of each day of our clean and sober time. You can create a building block this hour or a stumbling stone. The choice is yours.

This hour, I build a stepping stone of recovery by (check one) __going to a meeting, __calling my sponsor, __ calling a newcomer, __asking for guidance, __meditating a moment, __other.

Day Thirteen/6:00 PM: Sitting at a meeting and sharing how much you love everyone in the room is meaningless if you fail to help cleanup, talk to the newcomer, inquire after the old-timer, and make sure everyone has a ride home.

My well done is better than my well said.

Day Thirteen/7:00 PM: You don't wait and get well enough to do the steps; you do the steps to get well. This is the promise of our program, the rainbows of recovery: the Twelve Steps work.

Rainbows are the ribbons on God's gift to me, recovery

Day Thirteen/8:00 PM: "You gain strength, courage and confidence by every experience in which you really stop to look fear in the face. ...You must do the thing you cannot do." ~Eleanor Roosevelt

I do the thing I cannot do as I overcome F.E.A.R.
I Face Everything And Recover.

Day Thirteen/9:00 PM: When we suggest that newcomers call us anytime of the day or night because it helps us more than it helps them, we are not kidding. This is the essence of our Twelfth step work. "No one can sincerely try to help another without helping himself." ~Charles Dudley Warner

When I want to feel better right away,
I ask God to help me be of service.

Day Thirteen/10:00 PM: Don't let the therapeutically "correct" way to run a group hijack your meeting. Leaders are reluctant to cut a newcomer off for fear of shaming their inner child, rejecting them, or appearing to be mean. We are not therapy and we can't share with them if they can't listen.

I do not let the newcomer's inner child run our meetings. This is not play therapy.

Day Thirteen/11:00 PM: The Power behind us is greater than the problems in front of us.

Tonight, I am Higher Powered.

§

Day Fourteen/12:00 AM: Whether we think good things about ourselves or whether we think bad things about ourselves, mostly we are thinking about ourselves.

Although I keep the focus on myself, once the picture is taken, I move on.

Day Fourteen/1:00 AM: God, *as you understand him*: For the Atheist: Good Orderly Direction. For the Religious: Get Out Devil. For the Fellowship: Group Of Drunks. For working the Twelve Steps: Grow Or Die. For the newcomer: Grace Over Disease. For our daily reprieve: Grant One Day

It's not as important that I understand God, as it is that I understand there's a Power Greater than me.

Day Fourteen/2:00 AM: The word "humility" comes from "humus," which means earth or dirt. Humility *is the soil* in which all other virtues grow.

When I try to impress others with my growth, my halo becomes a noose!

Day Fourteen/3:00 AM: You are an evolving being and what you believe today, may not be what you believe tomorrow. If your conclusions about the world are set in concrete, when the world doesn't hold up to your mold, you will be furious at the "unfairness" of it all.

Like a child's Legos, my beliefs can be rearranged and rebuilt as I grow. The blocks that represented a rowboat at age four, became Battleship Galactica at age twelve.

Day Fourteen/4:00 AM: God does for you what you can't do for yourself. Your Higher Power does not do for you what you can do for yourself.

I only pray for potatoes, when I intend to pick up a hoe.

Day Fourteen/5:00 AM: When you start the day with quiet meditation, you create a consciousness of serenity and peace. At anytime during the day you can bring your mind back to this moment.

When things get hectic or stressful, I bring my awareness back to the peace that I create now.

Day Fourteen/6:00 AM: Try broadening your spiritual path by making your relationship with the Divine proactive. Ask not what the Universe can do for you, but rather what you can do for the Universe! Begin the morning with: *Hi World, what can I do for You today?*

Asking what I can do for the Creative Source will serve us both better than simply seeking what can be done for me.

Day Fourteen/7:00 AM: Since life is 10% actuality and 90% reactuality you must chose your reactions carefully. The program has given you choice and how you choose to react to this day can make the difference between simply being dry or being sober.

I live today as I want to remember my life.

Day Fourteen/8:00 AM: Although anger is usually seen as an "offensive" type emotion, us addicts actually use it as a "defense." When we focus on anger, we don't have to face ourselves. Anger can actually be understood as a form of defect denial by claiming that it's them, not us!

Anger is an acid that does more damage in the vessel that it is stored, than on anything it is poured!

Day Fourteen/9:00 AM: Deal with the small stuff or it will deal with you. Do not allow the small stuff to pile up on the camel's back. Take each situation that bothers you and deal with that as one unit, not as the straw that breaks the camel's back.

When I feel it, I deal with it and then can heal from it.

Day Fourteen/10:00 AM: It doesn't pay to argue with "slippers" about the proper way of getting clean and sober. Why should people who are still drinking and drugging tell those who are sober why it can't be done! We learn not to get in a pissing contest with a skunk. (or should we say drunk!)

The only thing I need to tell a drunk is how I got sober. I can't tell him or her how they will get sober, because I don't know.

Day Fourteen/12:00 PM: Being clean and sober doesn't mean we will lead a trouble free life. It simply means we might have a shot at doing something that won't make our troubles worse and might even make them better.

I pray not for a lighter burden but for a stronger back.

Day Fourteen/1:00 PM: A main theme in most spiritual traditions states that the best way to get what you want is to provide it for another. If you want serenity, make it peaceful and serene for another. Do you want a feeling of safety? Provide a safe place for another. Do you want to understand what has happened? Help another to understand.

I teach best what I most need to learn.

Day Fourteen/2:00 PM: If you have one hand in the fellowship and one hand in your Higher Power's, you can't pick up today.

I put my hand in my Higher Power's by saying. "Thy will not mine be done;" I put my hand in the fellowship by saying "I'll be there, at the next meeting."

Day Fourteen/3:00 PM: 90 meetings in 90 days is not nearly enough. Tell newcomers to always catch a ride or give a ride to their daily meeting. This way they get a meeting on the way to the meeting, a meeting during the meeting, and a meeting on the way home. That makes 270 meetings in the first 90 days!

Who am I taking to a meeting tonight?

Day Fourteen/4:00 PM: The life energy God gave us can be used anyway we choose. Compare it to electricity. You can plug a toaster into a socket and electricity will make toast *for* you. You can put your finger into the same socket and it will make toast *of* you.

I use the life energy entrusted to me for the growth of myself and others and not for the shock value.

Day Fourteen/5:00 PM: No one wants to hear the Sermon on the Mount or Zen philosophy when they're trying to save their ass. They want to know what to do—not hear words of wisdom. Tell them what you did.

I do not get so spiritual, that I am of no earthly value.

Day Fourteen/6:00 PM: Our Higher Power and recovery must come first or we stand in jeopardy of losing it all. The Maintenance Steps (Ten, Eleven, and Twelve) address this fully. We start the day with asking HP what to do, we spend the day doing it, and we end the day saying thank you.

I put my recovery first to make it last.

Day Fourteen/7:00 PM: Speak when you are angry and you will make the best speech you will ever regret.

I never trust my tongue when my heart is bitter.

Day Fourteen/8:00 PM: We often say, 'This too shall pass' when what we mean is 'You will pass through this just fine.' To get out of a difficulty, one usually must go through it.

I am not impatient with the universe—it sure hasn't been impatient with me!

Day Fourteen/9:00 PM: We are often surprised by who we can count on when the going gets tough. Someone we did not expect to come through might and others whom we thought we could count on may fall short of our expectations. We do not blame the ones that fall short and are grateful for the ones who go the extra mile.

I measure others by their best moments, not their worst.

Day Fourteen/10:00 PM: It is a monumental task to set your world in order as you make the changes necessary for spiritual growth. Setting your world in order does not mean to "fix" everybody and take care of their affairs. It means to tend to yourself and your affairs. Do not confuse "setting things in order" with controlling of others.

I do something for someone I love today, I leave them alone.

Day Fourteen/11:00 PM: Pissing contests about who used how much and who acted bad are ego trips in reverse. "It doesn't matter what or how much we used. In NA, staying clean has to come first. We realize that we cannot use drugs and live." (P 19, NA Basic Text).

When I brag about how much I used, how bad it was, and how much damage I did, I am doing one of two things, trying to make myself look larger or them smaller.

WEEK THREE

Day Fifteen/12:00 AM: Do not become one of these people who have two excuses for everything: one excuse for what you don't do and another for what you don't have.

Excuses are simply my lack of faith in me.

Day Fifteen/1:00 AM: It doesn't cost a lot of money for you to recover. It just takes everything you have.

As the pursuit of alcohol and drugs took all I had, so too does the pursuit of recovery.

Day Fifteen/2:00 AM: "Live and Let Live" sounds like a simple phrase, but in fact it is imperative for us to practice. When we try to control the actions of others, it only leads to anger, resentment, rage, and finally to a slip.

When I abused mind-affecting chemicals, I abused people and when I abused people, I abused mind-affecting chemicals. Today, I live my life and let others live their's.

Day Fifteen/3:00 AM: No God; No Peace. Know God; Know Peace.

My program teaches me that I will have peace of mind in the exact proportion of the peace of mind I bring into the lives of others.

Day Fifteen/4:00 AM: Even if our intentions are good, when we try to dominate the actions of others, we usually end up on a collision course with them. Tolerance is our path to harmony with our fellows.

I read pages 61, 62, & 63 in the book of Alcoholic's Anonymous when I catch myself telling others what they need to do.

Day Fifteen/5:00 AM: Don't push a newcomer to do the steps too fast. A heavy downpour runs off, whereas a gentle rain soaks in.

I don't drown the newcomer in program;
I irrigate them in patience.

Day Fifteen/6:00 AM: Many folks take the "live in today" to mean that we can't plan anything in the tomorrows. It's maddening to ask someone for lunch next week and they won't "commit" because "I live in today," they say. One of the promises of the program is to restore us to sanity and that means restore our ability to think clearly and make decisions.

I make all the plans I want, as long as I don't project the outcome. I plan, not project.

Day Fifteen/7:00 AM: Sponsors are lighthouses, not foghorns. We look to them to see how they do it, not depend on them to tell us what not to do. We already know.

I cannot improve if I only have myself as a model.

Day Fifteen/8:00 AM: We have been taught that the little white lie is OK because it keeps others from being hurt. We really don't know what will hurt another. Being dishonest with other people deprives them of the information they need to run their own lives.

Honesty is honesty. I understand that "little" dishonesties are a disservice to others as well as myself.

Day Fifteen/9:00 AM: Our program won't keep you from going to hell nor is it a ticket to heaven. But it will keep you clean and sober long enough for you to make up your mind which way you want to go.

My journey is my destination.

Day Fifteen/10:00 AM: Through the Fourth and Fifth steps we learn who we really are. Once we know who and what we are, we don't have to be what we were.

Today, I am myself. I am perfect for the part.

Day Fifteen/11:00 AM: If you keep doing the same thing over and over, you'll keep getting the same thing over and over. Doing one thing different, can make the difference.

Nothing changes if I change nothing!

Day Fifteen/12:00 PM: It matters not whether it's night time, day time, good times, or bad times, we only need to work this program thoroughly one time: NOW.

By working my program NOW, I turn my troubles around and WIN. NOW turned around is WON.

Day Fifteen/1:00 PM: Do not be afraid to seek advice and counsel from professionals trained in the addictions when needed. Psychologists, spiritual leaders, and medical practitioners are not romantically linked to our love affair with drugs. Therefore, their evaluation may be more nearly correct.

I do not discourage myself or others from seeking professional opinions when a situation warrants.

Day Fifteen/2:00 PM: When making amends, a subtle shift occurs in our thinking. We go from thinking we were a mistake to acknowledging we *made* a mistake.

I may make mistakes but my Higher Power doesn't and my Higher Power made me.

Day Fifteen/3:00 PM: Earth Angels dwell among us and they will find you at the moment you need them. These are the people who know just the right thing to say and do to keep you focused on recovery and principle.

Some of my Higher Power's best work is done anonymously.

Day Fifteen/4:00 PM: "Whenever a mind is simple, it is able to receive divine wisdom; old things pass away; it lives now and absorbs past and future into the present hour." ~Ralph Waldo Emerson

When I live in the now, the answers are simple and I can hear God thinking.

Day Fifteen/5:00 PM: "Each place along the way is somewhere you had to be to be here." ~Wayne Dyer

I cannot get ahead until I learn to be here.

Day Fifteen/6:00 PM: There is a certain universality to the truths taught in our Twelve-Step programs. They are nothing new. These principles are derived from eons of experience and spirituality. What is new is our personal understanding that *living* these principles gives us a reprieve from our addiction.

If I don't do it, I won't get it!

Day Fifteen/7:00 PM: Don't try, *let*. "If you will re-read the creation chapter in the Bible (the first of Genesis) you will notice that God creates by 'letting.' God said, 'Let there be light.' God said, 'let,' at every act of creation, and it was done.~ Someone said, 'Let go and let God,' and this is a wonderful recipe for overcoming fear...~ In any case, the rule for creation is always to *let*." ~Emmet Fox, *Find Inner Power*

The process is perfect; I let it work.

Day Fifteen/8:00 PM: We cannot rest on our laurels because the disease of addiction works through our subconscious and calls, "what do they know; just one won't hurt; well, if they're going to be like that!" Our subconscious pops silly excuses for abusing into our minds. We can always tell our addict inside, but we can't tell 'em much!

When I think I have a really really good idea, I run it by my sponsor first.

Day Fifteen/9:00 PM: Worry does not empty tomorrow

of its sorrow. It empties today of its strength.

I do no make today the tomorrow
I worried about yesterday.

Day Fifteen/10:00 PM: Resentment is from the Latin, meaning to "feel again." Rather than feeling *that* again, think of how it could have been worse, then be grateful it isn't. Once you get to the grateful part, you can't be resentful.

I cannot be grateful and resentful at the same time;
I can't serve two masters.

Day Fifteen/11:00 PM: Don't compare your insides to someone's else's outsides. You will always come up short. The only valid comparison is yourself to yourself over time.

Nothing about myself is to be feared;
I am only to be understood.

§

Day Sixteen/12:00 AM: You may reach a point where you feel that if one more person tells you "God won't give you more then you can handle," you'll blow up. Something you are going through *might* well be too much to handle; that is when you let God do for you what you can't do for yourself.

"I know God will not give me anything I can't handle. I just wish that He didn't trust me so much."
~Mother Teresa

Day Sixteen/1:00 AM: Being awake at one in the morning is not fun when you must face your demons alone. This is a good time to get out something inspirational to read, some meditation or prayer book, program text, scripture or even the lyrics of a favorite song.

I am not alone when I allow others to share through

the words they have written for me to read.

Day Sixteen/2:00 AM: If you pray, don't worry. If you worry, don't pray.

Thy will, not mine be done in and through me.

Day Sixteen/3:00 AM: Like the song says, "I'll bet you think this song is about you?" You need to get over yourself if you want to get over feeling sorry for yourself.

They're just doing it; they're not doing it to me.

Day Sixteen/4:00 AM: There will be times when you stew and fret over a careless thought that someone utters. They probably didn't mean to upset you and yet they did. All people say stupid or thoughtless things at times and so we treat them the way we would want them to treat us, if we made the mistake.

The biggest mistake I can make is not to recognize that I make mistakes.

Day Sixteen/5:00 AM: The AA Big Book, The NA Basic Text, and the CDA First Edition do not need to be rewritten. They need to be reread and reread.

I begin this day by reading at least one page from my program's basic book.

Day Sixteen/6:00 AM: It is characteristic of the humor in the Universe that we are given free will and then told to give it back! Be grateful for the choice. When you use, you don't have any.

I can choose to do right; I can choose to do wrong; with enough wrong choices, my choices will be gone.

Day Sixteen/7:00 AM: Unity in our program does not mean conformity. Unity means joining for a common purpose, despite our differences.

I can disagree without being disagreeable.

Day Sixteen/8:00 AM: The most important thing to know about Step Three, turning our will over to a Higher Power, is that all we can do is DECIDE to do it. There is no "will" we can wrap and send. Once we make the decision that we want to, it is basically done.

I decide to align my will with that of the Source of my Spirit.

Day Sixteen/9:00 AM: The Twelve Steps: One to Three: Clear up; Four to Nine: Clean up; Ten to Twelve: Contact up. These are also called the Foundation Steps, the Action Steps, and the Maintenance Steps respectively. Are you looking for something easier?

The easier, softer way is the Twelve Steps.

Day Sixteen/10:00 AM: We tell people, "Do the next right thing." Yet what is right? Often our mind tries to muddy our thinking by making excuses or rationalizing. Listen to your conscience—you really do know what is right.

I respond to the right and wrong of my Higher Self, not the "I want what I want" of self will.

Day Sixteen/11:00 AM: We do not believe in lemming recovery. Clement wrote "faith must go hand in hand with inquiry." If you do not "get" something, ASK. Ask at meetings, ask a clean and sober friend, ask your sponsor, or ask your Higher Power in prayer.

The only stupid question is the one I don't ask.

Day Sixteen/12:00 PM: Nothing is so bad that a drink or drug won't make it worse and nothing you have done is so bad that the Divine Source wouldn't be delighted to forgive.

I accept God's forgiveness by extending it to others.

Day Sixteen/1:00 PM: "You know that there is a way out

of any difficulty whatever, no matter what it may be, through the changing of your own consciousness by prayer. You know that by thus raising your consciousness any conceivable form of good that you can desire will be yours, and you know that nobody else can by any means hinder you from doing this when your really want to do it." ~Emmet Fox, *Getting Results by Prayer*

Nothing can hinder me from rebuilding my life because I believe in the power of prayer.

Day Sixteen/2:00 PM: Some members of the fellowship say "Our mind is a dangerous neighborhood to be in alone." But together we can be on block watch! Don't let your mind get the better of you. Turn that "M" in me upside down, like we are asked to *turn it over,* and make a "We" out of that "Me."

It isn't "me" and "you" anymore; it's "we" and "us."

Day Sixteen/3:00 PM: To become an old-timer: Don't drink; don't drug; don't die. With the Twelve Steps, you have a shot at living long enough to be old enough.

Time takes time.

Day Sixteen/4:00 PM: Our program will work for people who believe in God. Our program will work for people who don't believe in God. Our program will not work for people who believe they are God.

There is only one thing I need to know about my Spiritual Source, I am not He/She/It!

Day Sixteen/5:00 PM: Learning to be tolerant of others, a difficult task at best, does not mean that we have to agree with them! Tolerance disagrees agreeably, we think.

I came here demanding justice and I was graciously given mercy. I extend this mercy to my fellows when I find myself intolerant of their choices.

Day Sixteen/6:00 PM: You don't have to pretend to be someone you are not. You don't have to pretend to be strong (if you're a man) or fem (if you're a woman). You don't have to pretend that you don't want to use, if you do. Share what is real. The real you is enough.

I am enough; there is enough.

Day Sixteen/7:00 PM: You cannot think your way into a better way of living, but you can live your way into a better way of thinking.

I learn to act as if... and eventually
I'm not acting any more.

Day Sixteen/8:00 PM: Seemingly bad days are usually days when we don't get our own way.

Just for tonight, I adjust myself to what is, and
not try to adjust what is to myself.

Day Sixteen/9:00 PM: No matter how hard you attempt to control the people in your life, you will not find your fulfillment there. If they don't change, you will be frustrated; if they do change under your pressure, they will be frustrated.

If I look to others for fulfillment,
I will never be fulfilled.

Day Sixteen/10:00 PM: Occasionally you will blow it and hurt someone. Rather then try to make it up later, an immediate direct and sincere apology, in keeping with Step Ten, will keep you from building up more "stuff" to deal with. Try to live your life so you don't add to your Eighth Step list.

As I make amends for my outbursts, I listen
to their response without judgment.

Day Sixteen/11:00 PM: Do you have so many skeletons in the closet that you had to build a walk-in? Share the load. The AA Big Book says that, we "should be willing to bring former mistakes, no matter how grievous, out of their hiding places." (P 124) Not to do so is being self-centered and selfish.

I am only as sick as my secrets.

§

Day Seventeen/12:00 AM: Our feelings don't define us, our actions do. We are not bad because we have a quick temper--but we learn that expressing that anger hurts others. The longer we keep our temper the more it improves.

I am only as big as the smallest thing that makes me angry.

Day Seventeen/1:00 AM: You will be receiving many gifts from people in the programs: gifts of help, time, energy, possibly money, talents, and knowledge. You will never be able to pay them all back. You are not obligated to pay *them* back. You are obligated to pay them forward by giving away what you have when you can.

I appreciate the generosity of others and pay it forward when I am able.

Day Seventeen/2:00 AM: During crisis, we lean on each other. "There must be willingness to ask for, and to accept, the help of others. {~} If recovery could be achieved by ourselves, on our terms, we would not need this program." (P 107, CDA First Edition)

Before you decide you are too proud to be a member of this fellowship, make sure the fellowship would be proud to have you as a member.

Day Seventeen/3:00 AM: When egos collide, use kind words, do what you have control over, and do what you think is right. Surrender what you don't have control over, even if you think what others are doing is wrong.

Others have the right to be wrong.

I define myself by what I do and how I do it, not by who wins.

Day Seventeen/4:00 AM: Before our recovery we used people and loved things and given recovery we learn to love people and use things. Things are not important, people are.

I treat others the way I would be treated.

Day Seventeen/5:00 AM: Many people get the word "responsibility" confused with the word "control." They feel they have to fix this, take care of that, make that person see... and so on. Understand that "responsible" is not synonymous with "control" and doesn't require you to correct or fix anything, *unless you can*!

My responsibility is to respond to God's ability to run my life. I am responsible by responding with what I am able to.

Day Seventeen/6:00 AM: Who knows why they are chemically dependent? The answer will not change the fact, and yet many continue to question, why? Indeed, they need an answer, but they are asking the wrong question. The real question is, "How can I become free?" Free of the fear. Free of the pain. Free of the bondage.

I do not receive the right answer when I ask the wrong question.

Day Seventeen/7:00 AM: Humanity's greatest fear is the fear of death, physiologists tell us. Yet addict's fears run deeper. It is not death that contains our misery, but the dying that goes on while still alive.

The death of my addiction forces me to confront life.

Day Seventeen/8:00 AM: One hour at a time leads to one day at a time in our recovery program. Each hour is one of 24 building blocks of each day of our sobriety and clean time. My current building block is to be kind and considerate for this hour.

My one act of kindness can be the difference between a building block and a stepping stone.

Day Seventeen/9:00 AM: Our lives become very different once we learn to magnify our blessings the way we have our troubles.

What I think about enlarges. Am I enlarging my blessings or my troubles?

Day Seventeen/10:00 AM: "Forgiveness is not an occasional act; it is a permanent attitude." ~Martin Luther King. Undoubtedly, there are many on your list to forgive. There is only one whom you *must* forgive—that is yourself.

Because my Higher Power forgives me, I forgive myself.

Day Seventeen/11:00 AM: We find that the smallest deed is better than the grandest intention.

My actions speak louder than words. What are my actions saying now?

Day Seventeen/12:00 PM: If you have never experienced the results of working the Twelve Steps, no explanation is sufficient. If you have experienced the results of working the Twelve Steps, then no explanation is necessary.

I am the poster child for the miracles I cannot explain.

Day Seventeen/1:00 PM: When you continually don't like the way people treat you, it is usually because you are cooperating with the treatments.

The difference between me being a victor or a victim is ability. Response ability.

Day Seventeen/2:00 PM: We all experience moments seized by fear. Sometimes the fear is of something tangible, like fear of financial insecurity. It may be fear of the intangible, our own powerlessness. Your fear is a signal that you have to deal with some scary changes that have thrown you off kilter.

The only power fear has, is the power I give it. F.E.A.R. Face Everything And Recover

Day Seventeen/3:00 PM: "Often the answer is as simple as Step Twelve. We ask three questions: Am I paying attention to my spiritual needs? Am I passing on what I've received? Am I living in the principles I've come to hold dear? If the answer if 'no,' then we apply ourselves to the practice of this Step." (P 84, CDA First Edition)

I insure my sobriety, sanity, and serenity by practicing Step Twelve.

Day Seventeen/4:00 PM: An angry person doesn't even like himself.

When I feel anger, I identify the someone or something that isn't doing what I want and I give it up!

Day Seventeen/5:00 PM: "Step Ten frees us from the wreckage of our present. If we do not stay aware of our defects, they can drive us into a corner that we can't get out of clean." (P 41, NA Basic Text)

All my problems start out small. Dealing with them now ensures they will stay that way.

Day Seventeen/6:00 PM: People in our society stress that we ought to be happy. If you're not happy something is wrong, we are lead to believe. Yet, unhappiness is not a symptom of sickness, it is an expression of life, a natural reaction to situations we don't like. When shit happens, you don't have to like it.

I will not be unhappy about being unhappy.

Day Seventeen/7:00 PM: Going to a lot of meetings is

important, supportive, and full of fellowship. However, our program is not about meetings but what happens in between meetings.

Do I align my actions with the picture I paint of myself in meetings?

Day Seventeen/8:00 PM: The only difference between stumbling blocks and stepping stones is how you use them. No person, place, or thing can place blocks in your path if you chose to use them as steps.

I lift my feet as I use the blocks before me to (Twelve) Step up to the challenge.

Day Seventeen/9:00 PM: Sanskrit saying "God sleeps in the mineral, awakens in the plants, walks in the animals, and thinks in you." The Universal Source of life actually *thinks in you*. Use this well.

Every bad choice I ever made began with a single thought. Every good choice I ever made began with a single thought. I choose my thoughts carefully.

Day Seventeen/10:00 PM: Your thoughts and your prayers come from within, but your actions must be directed outward, to be of service. Transcending yourself, especially when you are obsessed with your own predicament, is the way to regain the meaning that will keep the meaning in your life.

I find that the " meaning" can be found under the ash trays.

Day Seventeen/11:00 PM: As these twenty-four hours draw to a close, we may feel anxious about what tomorrow will bring. But our program is a "**now**" program. Tomorrow will bring what tomorrow will bring, right now we're clean and sober!

If my Higher Power can handle eternity, I can surely handle right now!

§

Day Eighteen/12:00 AM: Another day of recovery begins and we start this day with surrender. "From that point, each of us is reminded that a day clean is a day won." (P 86, NA Basic Text)

When I surrender; I win.

Day Eighteen/1:00 AM: Some people cannot agree with the slogan that says, "Your worse day sober is better than your best day drunk" because they remember some jolly good times using and some sad times sober. What we can agree with, is that we are only one drink, fix, pill, toke, or line away from losing all we have found in our new way of life.

When I think of where I could be, I sure am happy to be where I am.

Day Eighteen/2:00 AM: How to share what it was like, what happened, and what it is like now. Be sincere. Be brief. Be seated.

When I share, I share to draw attention to the message, not the messenger.

Day Eighteen/3:00 AM: Just because we make mistakes doesn't mean we are failures. The only mistakes that become failures are the ones we don't learn from.

I have the right to be wrong.

Day Eighteen/4:00 AM: 'Resentment' is when you didn't get your way yesterday. 'Anger' is when you don't get your way today. 'Fear' is that you won't get your way tomorrow.

There are no good reasons for resentment, anger, and fear-- just good excuses.

Day Eighteen/5:00 AM: If you stop doing the things that keep you in the program, you will go back to doing the things that brought you to the program.

The price of my recovery is eternal vigilance.

Day Eighteen/6:00 AM: Our common bond binds us together and yet 'common bond' does not mean 'carbon copy.' Like the sun moving through a prism--you are a dancing ray of light among millions of lights. You are separate and yet connected to the whole.

I am a light from a prism not alight from a prison.

Day Eighteen/7:00 AM: God didn't do it!

God doesn't do anything to me, but always through me.

Day Eighteen/8:00 AM: Embrace all of your emotions for they are what make you, you. "Hold them in an embrace of total acceptance and in that embrace you will not be agonized any more. Do you think the Christ never cried? Do you think the Buddha never ached? You are not going to be less human, you are going to be wholly human." ~Bartholomew, *I Come as a Brother*

I become one with myself by embracing all of me,
because I am all of me and I won't be less!

Day Eighteen/9:00 AM: Pain is the difference between what is and what you would like it to be.

I can't change the wind, but I can adjust my sails.

Day Eighteen/10:00 AM: "When you ask for guidance and assistance, simply assume that it immediately is pouring forward. You may need to work a while to relax your mind into receptivity, or you may need to have lunch, or drive into town or do whatever it is that you need to do in order to relax your mind to hear or to feel, but live in the total assumption that the moment that you ask for guidance it is pouring in." ~Gary Zukav, *The Seat of The Soul*

Today, I trust the Universe.

Day Eighteen/11:00 AM: Do it right the first time. If you don't have the time to do something right, when will you have the time to do it over?

It takes less time for me to do something right, than to explain to my sponsor why I did it wrong.

Day Eighteen/12:00 PM: "Remember there's a very, very big world out there, with lots of loving people in it who you can have good relationships with." ~Toby Rice Drews. There are some relationships that you will never get back but that doesn't mean you won't have meaningful relationships

Rather than regret not having the relationships I would love to have today, I love the ones that HP would have me have today.

Day Eighteen/1:00 PM: The birth of resentment is blame. Often from the center of your bad feelings you seek someone to blame and yet if you "find" this someone, it can only serve to increase your misery. Blame increases misery because it gives you something to focus on again and again. "Resentment" is from Latin, meaning to "feel again."

By eliminating blame, I don't allow "them" to live rent free in my head.

Day Eighteen/2:00 PM: Sporadically, even with a strong program, you may feel spiritually dead or emotionally empty. We're addicts, it happens! No matter how dead or empty you sometimes feel, *this too shall pass.*

It came to pass… it didn't come to stay.

Day Eighteen/3:00 PM: We need to have our spiritual program replenished daily, because our recovery is "contingent on the maintenance of our spiritual program." Sometimes we need to replenish hourly.

This hour, I replenish my spiritual program by (check

one) __going to a meeting, __calling my sponsor, __ calling a newcomer, __asking for guidance, __meditating a moment, __other.

Day Eighteen/4:00 PM: We hug a lot. This can make newcomers uncomfortable because they are *not used* to being given love and attention without serious strings attached. By your example, you can teach them there are no strings to this love.

A hug is a great gift. One size fits all.

Day Eighteen/5:00 PM: "Every day, we have a choice about what kind of attitude we'll carry throughout the next 24 hours. Strike that and make it the next *hour*. We can't change the past. We can't change how people act or speak or think. We can, maybe, change the next hour or so by doing the right thing right now." ~Hal Ackerman, *Proverbs for Program People. Lessons for Life.*

I make a difference in this next hour by dong the right thing, right now.

Day Eighteen/6:00 PM: In light of your recovery, when dealing with family and friends, you may have to make some unpopular decisions and enforce them. Be open to moving toward the middle of issues that don't compromise your principles and going to any length for those that do.

My recovery is Twelve Steps past any lengths.

Day Eighteen/7:00 PM: Let go of any tendency you have to blame others for your unhappiness. You are a noble expression of God and must think of yourself with the same reverence that you would think of God. Would a Divine Source "blame" the tiger for attacking the gazelle or "blame" the atmosphere for the tornadoes that level homes or "blame" any process for being what it is?

I keep the focus on myself.

Day Eighteen/8:00 PM: Harold Kushner, author of *When Bad Things Happen To Good People* said that pain is the price we pay for being alive. So instead of wondering why we feel pain, more correctly we should ask, "What can I do to make my pain mean something more than suffering?"

No Pain; No Gain/Know Pain; Know Gain

Day Eighteen/9:00 PM: It is easier for us to blame others (parents, spouses, friends) for our predicaments then it is to look at self. Victims not only suffer pain, but they act as if someone else has the power to take that pain away.

The Blame Game is not a part of my recovery program.

Day Eighteen/10:00 PM: When you are having trouble doing one day at a time and it feels as though several days have attacked you at once, realize that nothing except your own thoughts can really attack. In fact, it is only your own thoughts that can prove to you that you have not been attacked or singled out unfairly.

I counter thoughts of "unfairness" with the realization that I am very lucky the world has not paid me back for all the wrongs I've caused.

Day Eighteen/11:00 PM: There may be a great temptation to believe that some sort of sacrifice is being asked of you when you are told you must accept reality. After all, isn't it reality that keeps messing up your fantasies? Do reality; it is the easier softer way.

Reality check: I am here "X"

§

Day Nineteen/12:00 AM: We alcoholics and addicts are disproportionate thinkers. It's the worst or it's the best; it's forever or it's never. Try moderation not magnification.

I needn't make a crisis out of an incident.

Day Nineteen/1:00 AM: Did you know that the word "share" derives from the Old English word for "shear" which means to cut or divide? To share with others means to divide your burden. Each time you share, you leave another little piece of the weight of your burden with them.

By sharing, I divide; by dividing, I lighten my load.

Day Nineteen/2:00 AM: Relapse is part of recovery: NOT! What the fellowships *say* is keep coming back SOBER." Members warn of the very real danger of that last relapse: stepping in front of a car or bus, overdosing, being institutionalized, and death! The truth is, any relapse can be your last. Never kid yourself, relapse is part of the disease process, not part of our recovery process.

I do not help people work on their recovery by
OKing working on their disease. OK

Day Nineteen/3:00 AM: Instead of saying "God will never give you more than you can handle" say, "God helps those who let Him do His job!" Your Divine Source, doesn't "give" you any burden to "handle." You are asked to do the right thing in the worst of circumstances and you are asked to practice the principles. Your Higher Power will "handle" the situation in the larger scheme of things.

I can't; He can; I think I'll let Him

Day Nineteen/4:00 AM: Whatever is disturbing you at this hour, stop for a moment and look around. What is the loveliest thing you see? Can you find your favorite color? What sound outside is from God's own creatures? Who can you think of right now that you love? Who loves you?

As I fill my head with positive thoughts,
it leaves no room for the negative.

Day Nineteen/5:00 AM: Your life works FOR you. It hones you, teaches you, and makes you a better person. Nothing in your life happens *to you*, but *for you.*

This isn't happening to me, but for me.

Day Nineteen/6:00 AM: Whether you are sober for 30 days or 30 years, be sure to tell others how they can support you. If you are new, group members may be reluctant to pressure you and if you are an old-timer they may feel inadequate to offer help. *Ask for what you need.* Those around you will appreciate it.

Asking draws solutions to me, and doesn't force those around me to guess.

Day Nineteen/7:00 AM: Recovery is not an event; it is a process. The disease of addiction affects all three aspects of our physical, mental, and spiritual selves by changing our behavior (to self-destruction), thinking (to self-serving), and allegiance (to no purpose). It was a slow debilitating process. Recovery is the same slow process in reverse.

I am in the process of changing my behavior to self-construction, my thoughts to service, and my allegiance from 'no purpose' to a higher purpose.

Day Nineteen/8:00 AM: Although we must be of service to our fellow drunk and junkie, although we want the hand of recovery to be there when they reach out, although we must give back what was so freely given to us, we cannot do for them what they must do for themselves.

I carry the message, I don't carry the drunk; however, if necessary, I carry the drunk to the message.

Day Nineteen/9:00 AM: If we knew what was best for us, there would be no need for Step Three. We can't see the whole picture from our limited view—there is

Someone else looking over us from a higher vantage point.

I am thankful for all that has been given to me, for all that has been taken from me, and all that has been left for me.

Day Nineteen/10:00 AM: Road rage and recovery rage are closely associated. People, places, and things get in our way and we freak. When the rage begins, quickly ask yourself, "What would my guardian angel do now?"

My DUI's are no longer under the influence of alcohol. Today, I Drive Unger the Influence of Angels.

Day Nineteen/11:00 AM: "There are no deals being offered here. You cannot trade the courage needed to live every moment for immunity from life's sorrows." ~Oriah Mountain Dreamer, *The Invitation.*

To gain that worth having,
it may be necessary to lose everything else.

Day Nineteen/12:00 PM: "Hope is trust in God even when everything seems hopeless. Hope is the assurance that God has the last word, and the word is life, even in the face of death." ~Foster R. McCurley and Alan G. Weitzman, *Making Sense Out of Sorrow, A Journey of Faith*

In the face of death, I lived. That is the
word of my Higher Power.

Day Nineteen/1:00 PM: Anger can be a source of personal power for people. When you get angry at God or others, even yourself, you feel the energy and you feel strong, not the helplessness of tears. Anger is a form of emotional denial.

Anger "may be the dubious luxury of normal men"
but it is not for me. (P 66, AA Big Book)

Day Nineteen/2:00 PM: Live as though everything you

do will eventually become known and you are living the program.

It is not the things I hide that will get me drunk;
it is the lying about the things I hide!

Day Nineteen/3:00 PM: Even though you are a unique human being, you are not so unique that your recovery is any different then thousands before you. If you think we don't understand something about your situation, then your disease is playing tricks on you.

I am unique, just like everyone else.

Day Nineteen/4:00 PM: Daily meditation for about 20 minutes is recommended for all in recovery, unless of course, you're very busy—then you should meditate for an hour.

May I be blessed with a slow recovery.

Day Nineteen/5:00 PM: Why me, why now? Once you stop analyzing *why*, you can ask the question that carries the solution in the asking. "What do I do now?" This question puts your focus in the present so you can live in the solution.

"Why" questions keep me in the problem while
"How" questions keep me in the solution.

Day Nineteen/6:00 PM: This is a good time to grasp the moment. No need to regret the past and what you did or didn't do; no need to contemplate the future for what "misfortunes" lay ahead. Simplify, simplify. Do you have laundry to wash? Can you fix a meal or call someone and go to a meeting? You can do that today.

I remember that it's a "cinch by the inch
and a trial by the mile."

Day Nineteen/7:00 PM: Life is like a tapestry. From the top it is a woven work of art, colorful images of beauty, yet on the other side it is a mishmash of jumbled threads. Are you absorbed with the top or the bottom of your tapestry?

When absorbed with the mishmash of threads that run through my life, I "turn it over" and view the patterns my Higher Power has woven for me.

Day Nineteen/8:00 PM: Take a breath and hold it. Take another and hold, hold, hold. You can see that you can't live on the inhale alone. The inhale is the breath of the program bringing you life. The exhale is you working with others.

I inhale healing for my soul and exhale hope for others.

Day Nineteen/9:00 PM: You can work the steps to *get* out of trouble or you can work the steps to *stay* out of trouble.

Change is mandatory, progress optional.

Day Nineteen/10:00 PM: In the words of Father Joe Martin, "You can lead a horse to water but you can't make them drink. But you sure as hell can make them thirsty!"

Just living my new, free life is often enough to make others "thirsty" for recovery. I don't always have to carry the message; I am the message.

Day Nineteen/11:00 PM: Any time you promise God that you will do "X" if "Y" happens, you are trying to strike a deal. God doesn't do deals. God allows you to dream, develop, and expand hand in hand.

I thank God for what I have,
I trust GOD for what I need.

§

Day Twenty/12:00 AM: We are responsible for what we do, no matter how we feel.

I cannot feel my way into better behavior, I must behave my way into better feelings.

Day Twenty/1:00 AM: Simple sleep is sometimes tough. Late at night the "what ifs" and "whys" rear their ugly heads. Activities cease and thoughts grow restless.

"Lord, unwrinkle my tired soul/unsnarl my garbled thoughts and words/unwind my gnarled nerves/and let me relax in thee". ~Marian Wright Edelman, Bedside Prayers

Day Twenty/2:00 AM: Friends and loved ones don't always behave as we expect them to. But this is a good thing. If friends and loved ones were absolutely predictable, that would mean they are not changing and if they are not changing, they are not growing.

I don't have to change friends if I understand that friends change.

Day Twenty/3:00 AM: Regardless of how long you have been clean and sober, there are times when the CD sickie that lives inside you will try to argue you back into picking up. It helps if you already know what you will answer, "There is no tragedy bad enough that a drink or drug won't make it worse and there is no success good enough that a toast won't toast me!"

I don't have to attend every argument I'm invited to.

Day Twenty/4:00 AM: Do you remember your childhood and the multitude of injustices that broke your tender heart? At times you may have blamed God, your parents, or yourself. Today with an adult perspective, you can see that you grew and gained despite your broken hearts, maybe because of them.

I view a broken heart like the hatching of an EGG (Experience, Growth, Gain); the shell has to break for the chick to begin a new life.

Day Twenty/5:00 AM: "If you understand, things are just as they are; if you do not understand, things are just as they are."~ Zen Proverb

I don't have to understand how the Steps work, just that they do.

Day Twenty/6:00 AM: There are some people who learn from the mistakes of others. Then there are the rest of us.

If I am not making mistakes, then I am probably not making anything.

Day Twenty/7:00 AM: They say that you need only one meeting a week but it might be a good idea to go to one every night so you don't miss the one you need!

Seven days without a meeting makes one weak.

Day Twenty/8:00 AM: "Drag your thoughts away from troubles…by the ears, by the heels, or any other way you can manage it. It's the healthiest thing a body can do." ~Mark Twain.

There is no trouble so bad that thinking about it won't make it worse.

Day Twenty/9:00 AM: "There is a principle which is a bar against all information. Which is proof against all arguments, which cannot fail to keep a man in everlasting ignorance. That principle is ---Comtempt prior to investigation." ~ Herbert Spencer

I do not reject things I know nothing about.

Day Twenty/10:00 AM: Egotism is that certain something that enables a man in a rut to think he's in a groove.

I am never in a rut when I can answer this question, "What Step am I working now?"

Day Twenty/11:00 AM: You will respect yourself to the degree that you do not violate your own value system.

Self-respect is the most important respect I can earn.

Day Twenty/12:00 PM: "You can either be a host of God or a hostage of your Ego." ~Wayne Dyer

E.G.O. Easing God Out

Day Twenty/1:00 PM: "Think of what you are doing as entering into partnership with Divine Intelligence, a partnership in which you begin to share your concerns with the understanding that there is an Intelligence receptive to what you're saying that helps you create within your own environment of matter and energy the most effective dynamics to bring you into wholeness." ~Gary Zukav, *The Seat of the Soul*

I share my concerns with Divine Intelligence.

Day Twenty/2:00 PM: Hugs, not drugs. Hugging can help establish a sense of security in us. Remember the Grandma and Grandpa hugs of your childhood? Allow others to bring back those feelings of comfort.

"Hug often. Hug well." ~Kathleen Keating,
The Hug Therapy Book

Day Twenty/3:00 PM: One of the quandaries that you may encounter in recovery is occasional feelings of envy for those who can still use alcohol, tranquilizers, and pain pills. It is the addict inside who provokes you. Next it'll be saying, "Why, if we could drink normally, we'd get drunk every night!"

I do not need to get in touch with my inner addict.
S/he is a sociopath.

Day Twenty/4:00 PM: A good listener is not only popular everywhere, but after awhile he knows something.

The next meeting I attend will be a "listen only" meeting.

Day Twenty/5:00 PM: Conflicts are a part of reality.

"We learn not to become emotionally involved with problems. We deal with what is at hand and try not to force solutions. We have learned that if a solution isn't practical, it isn't spiritual." (P 87, NA Basic Text)

I do not fix problems. I do the right thing and allow the solution to evolve.

Day Twenty/6:00 PM: They say our character defects are like an onion. They come off in layers and make us cry as they peel away. For each shortcoming we address, new realizations and perceptions bring us new layers and levels.

New Level, New Devil.

Day Twenty/7:00 PM: At times, the future might look bleak and normalcy seem hopeless. Yet you've been in despairing situations before and something unexpected happened, then *everything changed.* Remember that things can change in ways you can't possibly anticipate.

I remain open to new potentiality.

Day Twenty/8:00 PM: Dishonesty is like a boomerang. About the time you think all is well, it hits you in the back of the head.

"Does what I gain by lying really balance out the integrity I lose?" (P 54, CDA First Edition)

Day Twenty/9:00 PM: Demonstrate your capacity for compassion and the Divine Forces will demonstrate compassion for you. It is a law of the universe. Right now, think of the still suffering chemically dependent and spend 60 seconds in prayer for them

I send my light and love to the still suffering alcoholic and addict.

Day Twenty/10:00 PM: You needn't look at the world as something that needs to be improved upon and fixed by you. You are, in fact, what God is doing with this world. You! And everything that goes into shaping you is perfect, including what you think is not.

I am the work of this Universe. God doesn't make junk.

Day Twenty/11:00 PM: Recovery takes place with every breath. And like your breath, you don't really notice the progress. It goes on n the background of your life, but your *life depends on it*. Stop breathing and you notice immediately you need air; stop recovering and you notice immediately you need a program.

I inhale light, exhale dark. I inhale recovery, exhale despair.

§

Day Twenty-one/12:00 AM: "Loneliness and the feeling of being unwanted is the most terrible poverty." ~Mother Teresa. In our fellowships, you never have to be lonely again.

When I am alone, it does not mean I am lonely. Lonely is a choice.

Day Twenty-one/1:00 AM: To a practicing addict who lives wholly in the sensations of the body, the recovery state is one of utter boredom. But as we learn to live balanced in body, mind, and soul, we wonder why we ever thought the state of addiction exciting.

Sometimes I get rebellious. Sometimes I get bored. But I just don't pick up.

Day Twenty-one/2:00 AM: Spend a few moments praying whenever feelings overwhelm you. If you don't believe in prayer, call it meditation. If you don't believe in meditation, call it listening to the silence. Whatever you call it, just do it.

Every good thought is a prayer.

Day Twenty-one/3:00 AM: "Just exactly what can we do to put our spiritual principles into practice? Here are some ideas. We can say *love* when others say *hate*. We can say *people* when others say *money*. We can speak up when others are silent. We can carry on when others give up. We can offer help when others withdraw." ~Anonymous, *Day By Day*

I practice these principles in all my affairs--
or change my affairs.

Day Twenty-one/4:00 AM: Enthusiasm was originally a Greek word that meant "a god within." With your "god within," you can meet any situation with dignity and grace.

I greet the morning with 'enthusiasm' for all that I am
and all that I may become today.

Day Twenty-one/5:00 AM: Success is never fatal. Failure is never final.

If I never fail, it's because I never risk.

Day Twenty-one/6:00 AM: What the Devil presents to you is always a real pretty picture. But there is always one hellava price to pay.

No one is easier to deceive than myself.

Day Twenty-one/7:00 AM: "We must never forget that we may also find meaning in life when confronted with a hopeless situation, when facing a fate that cannot be changed. For what then matters is to bear witness to the uniquely human potential at its best, which is to transform a personal tragedy into a triumph." ~Viktor E. Frankl, *Man's Search for Meaning*

God, grant me the courage to change the things I can.

Day Twenty-one/8:00 AM: "Each day has its own set of thoughts, words and deeds. Live in tune." ~Rebbe

Nachman of Breslov

"Nothing can stop me from growing today."
~SpiritLifters

Day Twenty-one/9:00 AM: Meetings will not keep you sober but they sure as heck will mess up your drinking and drugging. People with a belly full of booze and head full of program find it a miserable way to live.

I may have one more drunk left inside, but not another sobering up—I don't take any chances.

Day Twenty-one/10:00 AM: "We need courage to meet what comes and know that whatever it is, it will not last forever." ~Leo F. Buscaglia.

My problems are guidelines, not stop signs.

Day Twenty-one/11:00 AM: Each day is a new beginning that offers you the opportunity to practice new skills, perceptions, and behaviors. This makes you a beginner.

My new life today, makes me a beginner. I am as gentle with myself as I would be with any beginner.

Day Twenty-one/12:00 PM: Practice faith, not fury in the ways of the world. Let go. Letting go simply means allowing for the fact that the world runs with or without your consent. It means *deciding* to have faith, not fury in the ways of the world.

I place myself in the middle of the stream of power that runs the universe. I practice faith, not fury, in the ways of the world.

Day Twenty-one/1:00 PM: Addiction is a living death. Defy it.

"My defiance about death awakens me to my love of life."
~Pat Samples, Daily Comforts for Caregivers

Day Twenty-one/2:00 PM: Do not project into the future how things are going to be. Tomorrow is today's mystery.

If you project a continuum of pain and failure, you only invite that pain and failure. Allow the world to surprise you, because it surely will.

Tomorrow is today's mystery as today becomes tomorrow's history. I do not write more pain and failure into my history books.

Day Twenty-one/3:00 PM: Take time to laugh, for "we think that cheerfulness and laughter make for usefulness." (P 132, AA Big Book). Resolve today to watch a movie or comedy routine for the sole purpose of laughing--not to learn, not to help others, not to do the right and dutiful thing, just for the heck of it.

Today, I find and watch one film, video, movie, or TV show that makes me laugh.

Day Twenty-one/4:00 PM: "Exhaust the little moment. Soon it dies./And be it gash or gold it will not come/Again in this identical disguise." ~Gwendolyn Brooks, *Exhaust the little moment*

This moment is the Universe's gift to me. What I do with it is my gift to the Universe.

Day Twenty-one/5:00 PM: Stumbling blocks become stepping stones when we use each adversity as a chance to practice our new way of life. Problems become challenges as we discover what part of our program to apply. What principle can you apply to your current situation?

I am still as I ask my inner guidance what principle to apply to the situation I find myself in.

Day Twenty-one/6:00 PM: "This life's five windows of the soul,/ distorts the Heavens from pole to pole,/ and leads you to believe a lie, / When you see with, not thro', the eye." ~William Blake. It is by looking *through* the windows of the soul you find the understanding of what your life presents, not by seeing with your physical eyes what is or isn't on the earth.

I close my eyes in order to "see" what my Higher Power presents to me.

Day Twenty-one/7:00 PM: Chemically Dependant Anonymous' First Edition says, "{Our program}is founded on the principle that our common experience, of both dependence and recovery, provides us with unique opportunities to help others like us, and in the act of helping, we ourselves stay clean and sober and growing. Therefore carrying the message is vital." (P 81)

Working with others is my real work.
The Twelve Steps are my preparation for that.

Day Twenty-one/8:00 PM: All our suggestions are free. The ones you don't take are the ones you end up paying for.

"Clean and sober" is not a sentence; it is a reprieve.

Day Twenty-one/9:00 PM: When you are the sponsor and not the sponsee, how do you expect your sponsee to behave? Are you acting in a manner consistent with what you believe is right with your own sponsor?

I act in a manner with my sponsor as I would have my sponsees act with me.

Day Twenty-one/10:00 PM: Humility is being a part of the whole not apart from the whole.

My humility is my humanity.

Day Twenty-one/11:00 PM: If you don't believe in prayer, believe anyway. *Prayer is Powerful.* Whatever your Spiritual Source may be, God, Group, or Goodness, use the power of prayer to strengthen and guide you.

I clasp my hands in prayer, and like a plug into a socket, I tap into the power of the Universe.

WEEK FOUR

Day Twenty-two/12:00 AM: Do not be satisfied to drift with the currents, hoping that somehow, somewhere all will work out. Take action. Do not put off today what you can do tomorrow.

I grow as a result of my efforts, not my complacency.

Day Twenty-two/1:00 AM: The sole purpose of AA is to help the alcoholic stop drinking. The sole purpose of NA is to help the addict stop using. The sole purpose of CDA is to help the chemically dependent give up mind affecting chemicals. The soul purpose of all these fellowships is service, unity, and recovery.

"I do not put the sole purpose of any fellowship above the soul purpose." ~Shelly Marshall

Day Twenty-two/2:00 AM: Believe those who are seeking the truth. Doubt those who have found it. There are no gurus in our fellowships.

I do not tie my ego up in being an "old-timer" or being a fellowship guru.

Day Twenty-two/3:00 AM: In prayer, "We can use words or we can pray silently through careful, mindful, spiritual acts. We can pray for ourselves or others, for what we need or want, or we can pray to follow the will of our Higher Power. In fact, we can make a prayer out of most anything we do. The way we do what we do can make most any act a prayer." Anonymous, *Day By Day*

Through mindful, spiritual acts, I become a living prayer.

Day Twenty-two/4:00 AM: Programming positive attitudes and behaviors into our new life isn't exactly easy and can't be done yesterday. If we have been drinking and using two times a day for five years, that's 4,150 negative reinforcements to be overcome!

My Higher Power is greater than my past: more cunning, baffling, powerful and patient!

Day Twenty-two/5:00 AM: Emmet Fox writes of the Golden Key that will solve every trouble or confusion. "Stop thinking about the difficulty, whatever it is, and think about God instead." Nothing else need be done. Whenever a situation arises, replace the negative thoughts or worries with thoughts of your Higher Power and you will be amazed how things work out by themselves.

I "Golden Key" the next person, place, or thing, that troubles me tonight.

Day Twenty-two/6:00 AM: When you go to meetings, you will see that "they" accept their lot in life; "they" go about their business each day; "they" are thankful for their blessings; "they" are willing to rely on a Higher Power; "they" are happy and working with others.

I used to resent "they." Now I am one.

Day Twenty-two/7:00 AM: How to get honest: If it's not yours—don't take it. If it's not true—don't say it. If it's not right—don't do it.

I don't have the capacity to be honest, I make the capacity to be honest.

Day Twenty-two/8:00 AM: People say, "Call me anytime." That is not just for newcomers. "The still suffering alcoholic" can be you at any stage of recovery.

I am never hopeless or helpless as long as I keep handy, a phone list of people in the fellowship.

Day Twenty-two/9:00 AM: The only time we should look down on anyone is when we are bending over to help them up.

When anyone, anywhere reaches out for help...

Day Twenty-two/10:00 AM: One sure way to stay focused on the negative is to try to find who is to blame. Once you find that person, then you can spend lots of time trying to make them pay for the suffering they have caused you. Or, you can work Step Three.

I no longer consider it my duty to set things right.

Day Twenty-two/11:00 AM: All of us go through phases of loving meetings, hating meetings, or ambivalence. Buddha said that in this life we would experience ten thousand joys and ten thousand sorrows. He understood that emotions ride on the currents of life.

My recovery rides on the currents of life and as long as I don't pick up, I can never drown in my sorrows!

Day Twenty-two/12:00 PM: Don't "but" your program around. "Yes, but.." means you don't mean yes. "I'm working the step, but.." means you are not working the step. Everything after the word "But" cancels out everything before it.

I put my "buts" where they belong, in the ashtrays or the seats at meetings.

Day Twenty-two/1:00 PM: No matter what you are doing, slow down, breathe, and be still now. Whatever is troubling you, you have the resources to work through it. "The teacher is within, so you have to learn to be still...you have to learn to live your life so that you are listening within, no matter what you are doing." ~Bartholomew, *I Come as a Brother*

I pause, breathe deeply, and listen for the guidance of my own teacher-self.

Day Twenty-two/2:00 PM: It is important for us to think in the positive. It doesn't help to think "I don't want to use, I don't want to lose," because we end up thinking of what we *don't want*. We energize that very thing. If we think, "I like having a clear mind; I like remembering; I like growing," we have positive thoughts directed away from our disease.

My thoughts focus on what I'm working toward,
not what I'm escaping from.

Day Twenty-two/3:00 PM: People who judge other people for not doing what they say they are doing are usually not doing what *they* say they are doing.

If I'm taking another's inventory, who will take mine?

Day Twenty-two/4:00 PM: Our disease is not the drug; it is a system malfunction in the body. This malfunction is in the brain (neurochemistry), in the mind (irrationality), and in the spirit (immorality). Only by healing all three do we have any hope of recovering.

I do not fight the chemicals that made me sick; I fight the malfunctions that make me want to use them.

Day Twenty-two/5:00 PM: "In accordance with the principles of recovery, we try not to judge, stereotype or moralize with each other." (P 11, NA Basic Text)

I take care of my heart. I do not run up hill
and I don't run down people.

Day Twenty-two/6:00 PM: We can't always choose where or what we are in life, but we can choose how to view it. Adversity can be seen as an opportunity to work our spiritual program. We find that when one door is closed to us, another one invariably opens.

I choose to see my coffee cup as half full
rather than half empty.

Day Twenty-two/7:00 PM: "A note of music gains significance from the silence on either side." ~Anne Morrow Lindberg

God gave me a mouth that closes and ears that don't.

That should tell me something.

Day Twenty-two/8:00 PM: We have a lot to recover and a lot to recover from: economic, marital, parental, employment, religious, and legal. Some pop psychology fads may try to pick one or two of these areas and act as if working on that will "cure" us. Our continuing recovery is not connected to a good marriage, job, or other "thing."

My recovery is connected to principle;
not people places or things!

Day Twenty-two/9:00 PM: Your thoughts are the foot prints in the wet cement of today. They make the impressions that "set" in your tomorrow's. Observe your thoughts and how they impact your tomorrow's. Are you telling yourself things that will harden into stumbling stones or building blocks?

As I work Step Eleven, I carefully review not only my actions, but my thoughts. Unconstructive thoughts, I now correct.

Day Twenty-two/10:00 PM: Compulsive behavior is characterized by the need to be better than, sooner than, bigger than, more than.... This creates pressure which creates stress, which for us creates danger! That is why we take the slogan "Easy Does It," seriously.

I do it easy (but I do it).

Day Twenty-two/11:00 PM: If you let other people do it for you, they invariably will do it to you.

I do not let others do for me what I can do for myself.

§

Day Twenty-three/12:00 AM: When you can't find the solution to a problem, look for the soulution to the problem.

I keep whispering my heart's desires because I never

know when my angel is listening.

Day Twenty-three/1:00 AM: If you are clean and sober, the miracle has already happened. Stick around, the impossibilities take a little longer.

Nothing is impossible in God's world.

Day Twenty-three/2:00 AM: The reason people blame other people is because there is only one alternative.

I do not point a finger at another because there are always three pointing back at me.

Day Twenty-three/3:00 AM: Recovery is an attribute of two personalities which bear a relationship one to the other. This is our self and our higher self or God-self. There are two of us: self and God-self. We do not walk this path alone.

I used to be self and drug-self.
Now I am self and God-self.

Day Twenty-three/4:00 AM: It is remarkable how often we run across this feeling of "uniqueness" as we recover. We may brag that we used more, had worse contacts, spent more in bars, treated our family worse, were younger, older, blacker, gayer, more sensitive--whatever.

I am the only 'me' there is ever going to be. I do not try to convince others that I am a better me than they.

Day Twenty-three/5:00 AM: "Someone once joked that the whole point of time is to keep everything from happening at once. The time is now. And life, then, is an unbroken series of nows. If you really want to get the most out of the here and now, don't waste it by reliving other times, good or bad." ~Hal Ackerman, C.D.T. *Wearable Parables*

I add life to my years and years to my life by not wasting my time reliving other times.

Day Twenty-three/6:00 AM: The slogans may sometimes annoy us in their simplicity, but can be an important tool in our fight for survival. 'Slogan' is an old Scottish word for "War Cry" and war cries give us courage going into battle.

My favorite 'war cry' for survival today is ______.

Day Twenty-three/7:00 AM: Everyone has problems. Your problem though, is not the real problem. The *real problem* is how you deal with the original problem.

I work the program, not the problem.

Day Twenty-three/8:00 AM: "The present moment is never intolerable. It is always what is coming in five minutes or five days that makes people despair. The Law of Life is to live in the present, and this applies to both time and place. Keep your attention to the present moment, and in the place where your body is now." ~Emmet Fox, *Around Emmet Fox*

I learn to Be Here Now so I can

Free There Then

Day Twenty-three/9:00 AM: We came to the Twelve Step fellowship to save our ass, and found out our soul was attached. It doesn't mean our answers are in religion. But they are in our spirituality.

I make believe until I can believe.

Day Twenty-three/10:00 AM: It helps to learn the difference between being responsible to others and being responsible for others. It helps for them to learn the same thing!

Powerless over people, places, and things is a two-way street.

Day Twenty-three/11:00 AM: As you sponsor others, remember this: If you are trying to recreate someone in your own image, then one of you will be redundant.

My job as a sponsor is to model,
not mold, recovery for my sponsees.

Day Twenty-three/12:00 PM: "Truth has no special time of its own. Its hour is now—always, and indeed then most truly when it seems most unsuitable to actual circumstances." ~Zwischen Wasser und Urwald , *On the Edge of the Primeval Forest*

I prevent truth decay—by brushing up on
my maintenance Steps every day.

Day Twenty-three/1:00 PM: There is a mediation/prayer of loving kindness from the Buddhist practice of "metta," that is presented by Wayne Muller in *Legacy of the Heart*. This is designed to send loving kindness to *yourself*. You may want to incorporate this into your practice of Step Eleven. Settle into a safe place; say these words to yourself slowly,

"May I dwell in the heart. May I be healed. May I be
filled with love. May I be free from suffering.
May I be happy. May I be at peace."

Day Twenty-three/2:00 PM: It's hard work taking everyone else's inventory. Worst of all, they seldom seem grateful!

When I concentrate on myself, I don't have
time to find fault with others.

Day Twenty-three/3:00 PM: When we feel that fate has dealt us a bad hand with chemical dependency, we simply remember that many people have MS, cancer, diabetes, lupus, or a myriad of maladies that are not so easily put into remission.

Because I count my blessings, my blessings count.

Day Twenty-three/4:00 PM: We are the inheritors of those who have gone before us, the originators of the

Twelve Step programs. Their blood, sweat, tears, and persistence is a gift to us. Their sheer tenacity in educating the public, the government, the medical profession, and most of all themselves is our great legacy.

I carry forth the legacy one principle at a time,
one day at a time, one hour at a time.

Day Twenty-three/5:00 PM: When they ask for a topic at tonight's meeting, suggest "What Happens to People Who Don't Go to Meetings?"

If I don't go to meetings, I won't hear what
happens to people who don't go to meetings.

Day Twenty-three/6:00 PM: There is nothing about you that was not intended to be. You have an incredibly sacred purpose.

I am on purpose.

Day Twenty-three/7:00 PM: Some program members get stuck on rules of what one can and can't say and what dependency qualifies one to be in what recovery group. They demand that newcomers follow traditions *as interpreted by them*. This can drive newcomers away before they even find out what recovery means.

I carry the message, not the mess.

Day Twenty-three/8:00 PM: What is it that makes people suppose they can more easily do twice tomorrow what they didn't do once today? Just do it.

I begin: the rest is easy.

Day Twenty-three/9:00 PM: You have to give it away to keep it. Our co-founders grasped this principle from the beginning. It is written on page 20 of the Big Book, "Our very lives... depended upon our constant thought of others..." and on page 153 "... give of yourself that others may survive,,," It is by helping others that we save ourselves.

By giving it away, I get to keep it.

Day Twenty-three/10:00 PM: In working with others, remember that no one cares how much you know, until they know how much you care.

I love the unloveables.

Day Twenty-three/11:00 PM: We hear so much about spiritual principles. What are they? A spiritual principle is a standard of conduct by which we remain right with the world. Some of these are: honesty, integrity, kindness, accountability, service to others, and good humor.

When I want to know what principle to practice in a situation, I ask myself, what would my sponsor do?

§

Day Twenty-four/12:00 AM: We learn when working with others that if they're not ready to learn, we can't say anything right. And if they're ready to learn, we can't say anything wrong.

When the pupil is ready, the teacher appears and sometimes it happens to be me!

Day Twenty-four/1:00 AM: It is written in the Big Book regarding our past, that we "should be willing to bring former mistakes, no matter how grievous, out of their hiding places." (P124). We are only as sick as our secrets.

I am only as healthy as my honesty.

Day Twenty-four/2:00 AM: "The minute you ask for vision, for release, for understanding, for peace of heart in the midst of difficulties; when you no longer ask that they be removed by some Big Daddy, but stay with them because they are there, you will realize that your present difficulty is only a small part of you, and the rest is doing very well, thank you." ~Bartholomew, *I Come as a*

Brother

The rest of me is doing very well, thank you!

Day Twenty-four/3:00 AM: When things get easy, it's easy to stop growing.

When I'm through changing, I'm through.

Day Twenty-four/4:00 AM: "This is the essence of spirituality: connection with sources of strength, and most of all with a power greater than ourselves." (P 80, CDA First Edition)

When I place spiritual values first in my life,
everything else falls into place.

Day Twenty-four/5:00 AM: How long does it take to clear away the wreckage of our past? In the Northwest region of the U.S., Native Americans have a special saying, "How long does it take to clear a landslide? One rock at a time."

I remove the landslide of my past, one rock at a time.

Day Twenty-four/6:00 AM: The key to success is not to *will* anything to happen, but to simply be willing. As your Higher Self oversees your circumstances, you will be drawn to the new experiences that are part of your future. Forcing solutions may call forth experiences before you are ready.

I am willing to accept my future,
but I don't will my future into being.

Day Twenty-four/7:00 AM: "There are only 24 hours in the day; every 24-hour period is the canvas with which I work. Every time I tap into 10 seconds of a good feeling is 10 seconds I can't be feeling a bad one. They add up." ~Anne Wayman *Powerfully Recovered*

My smile puts the wrinkles in the right places.

Day Twenty-four/8:00 AM: If you have been doing

anger too long, self-pity too long, or any negative emotion too long, it is time to switch emotions. The best way to switch is through random acts of kindness. Send flowers to a lonely neighbor--with no name attached; give your neighbor's cat a cat nip toy; take down all the outdated messages on the community bulletin. It works.

I change anger to serenity and self-pity to pride through a random (and anonymous) act of kindness.

Day Twenty-four/9:00 AM: It is all too easy to reject the suggestions of the program, people in the program, and even this pocket book. You may find practical and solid reasons for abandoning each opportunity to break out of the cycles of self-absorption. Yet your emptiness will increase with each missed opportunity.

It is just as easy for me to find practical and solid reasons to accept helpful suggestions as it is to reject them.

Day Twenty-four/10:00 AM: Some people disguise procrastination using the word "patience." Procrastination is fear in five syllables. Patience is faith in two.

What I "have accomplished is only a matter of willingness, patience and labor." (P 163, AA Big Book)

Day Twenty-four/11:00 AM: Pure and simple: Fear is the absence of Faith. Whether your fears are the *Frantic Efforts to Appear Recovered* or the *F*ck Everything And Run* type, one thing is guaranteed to alleviate them, the *Fear Ain't In This House* type of faith..

My fear no longer owns me.

Day Twenty-four/12:00 PM: Taking Step One does not mean you are powerless—just powerless over alcohol, mind-affecting mood-altering chemicals, and addiction. This does not mean that you have no power. Indeed, you have the power, *must exercise the power*, to work the rest of the steps.

I am powerless over my addiction but not my program.

Day Twenty-four/1:00 PM: Which “isms” affect you? Alcoholism: Incredibly Short Memory. Egoism: I, Self, and Me. Recidivism: I Sponsor Myself. Narcissism: InSide Me. Pessimism: I Sabotage Myself. Optimism: Incredibly Spiritual Moments.

Which “ism” do I adopt for my life?

Day Twenty-four/2:00 PM: Your Divine Source will always answer your prayers. Sometimes the answer is "no" but we still cry, "HP didn't give me what I wanted so HP doesn't listen to me." The Divine listens, maybe you don't.

I ask and wait for the answer. If I don’t get an answer, that’s the answer.

Day Twenty-four/3:00 PM: Every morning that you wake up, you have a choice. You can choice to use, or not. Once you use, though, you no longer have a choice.

Once I choose to use, I can no longer use my choice.

Day Twenty-four/4:00 PM: In the fellowship, our means of support are each other. However, when others look at us, they do not *see* what we *feel*. Just because our needs are so glaring to us, doesn’t mean they are obvious to others.

I take the time to explain what’s going on with me so I don’t expect the fellowship to provide invisible means of support.

Day Twenty-four/5:00 PM: Your imagination is a powerful tool. Research has shown that pitchers who “imagine” themselves making perfect throws actually improve their game. Now is the time to imagine yourself flourishing and happy in the future.

I envision myself as happy, sober and me.

Day Twenty-four/6:00 PM: Life is not black or white. It's black *and* white. And zillions of colors in-between. To understand this is to understand the magnificent rainbow of your life.

By reading the black and white pages of the AA Big Book (CDA First Edition or NA Basic Text), I color my life beautiful.

Day Twenty-four/7:00 PM: In recovery, the years go by quickly. It is the individual days that we have trouble with. That is one reason why this has to be a daily program.

I can do anything for 24 hours.

Day Twenty-four/8:00 PM: "Whether one believes in a religion or not, and whether one believes in rebirth or not, there isn't anyone who doesn't appreciate kindness and compassion." ~The Dalai Lama

When I do good, I never know how much good I do.

Day Twenty-four/9:00 PM: Engage your soul. Whether you use prayer, church, meditation, read recovery texts, take long walks, use Eastern philosophies, martial arts, or spiritual fellowship--your soul must be engaged for you to grow.

I ensure my sobriety, sanity, and serenity by engaging my soul in my recovery.

Day Twenty-four/10:00 PM: The law of physics says there is only one way to coast: down hill.

If I am not moving forward, I am moving backward. There is no coasting in recovery.

Day Twenty-four/11:00 PM: "I am a survivor of four camps --concentration camps, that is-- and as such I also bear witness to the unexpected extent to which man is capable of defying and braving even the worst conditions conceivable." ~Viktor E. Frankl, *Man's Search for Meaning.*

I possess all the courage I need to meet all the challenges life presents.

§

Day Twenty-five/12:00 AM: Some of us change when we see the light, most of us change when we feel the heat. Are you waiting to get burned before you do what you need to?

If I don't change... my clean and sober date will.

Day Twenty-five/1:00 AM: "It's only when we truly know and understand that we have a limited time on earth -- and that we have no way of knowing when our time is up, we will then begin to live each day to the fullest, as if it was the only one we had."-- Elisabeth Kubler-Ross

Today is the first day of the rest of my life and I give it the mindfulness it deserves.

Day Twenty-five/2:00 AM: They say, "When all else fails, read the directions." In recovery, we say, "When all else fails, only *then are you ready* to read the directions." It takes what it takes.

I do not wait to hit the bottom of a problem before I hit the books for directions.

Day Twenty-five/3:00 AM: "Never bear more than one kind of trouble at a time. Some people bear three--all they have had--all they have now--and all they expect to have." ~Edward Everett Hale

"The worst things I ever lived through never happened." AA Grapevine, April 2000, P 7.

Day Twenty-five/4:00 AM: There is no completion for the circle of recovery. A circle has no beginning and no end. It is suggested that recovery begins when you have learned enough from those before you and pass it along to those behind. Love is the process that keeps the circle moving.

Standing hand in hand or arm in arm after a meeting I absorb the love that travels our circle of recovery.

Day Twenty-five/5:00 AM: You may delve into the spiritual and find yourself, or you may delve into yourself and find the spiritual. The beauty of our steps is that they are designed to cover all bases.

I contemplate my soul in Step Five, I look to the stars in Step Eleven; I find my sacred self.

Day Twenty-five/6:00 AM: At the start of meeting we always ask, "Is there anybody new or coming back?" We should also ask, "Is there anybody old and going out?"

I remember that the "still suffering alcoholic" can include old timers too!

Day Twenty-five/7:00 AM: "The turning point in the process of growing up is when you discover the core of strength within you that survives all hurt." ~Max Lerner. That "core of strength" is based on abstinence and spiritual principles.

I suit up; I show up: I grow up.

Day Twenty-five/8:00 AM: The consequences of being dishonest, of being a liar, is not so much that others will not believe you, as it is that you can not believe others.

"Does what I gain by lying balance out the integrity I lose?" (P 54, CDA First Edition)

Day Twenty-five/9:00 AM: The smallest deed is better than the grandest intention. The smallest kindness is better than the best pitch.

It's nice to be important but it's more important to be nice.

Day Twenty-five/10:00 AM: Sarah Ban Breathnach,

author of *Simple Abundance* writes "When we offer thanks to God or to another human being, gratitude gifts us with renewal, reflection, reconnection... every time we remember to say 'thank you' we experience nothing less than Heaven on earth."

I say "Thank You" not because they need to hear it, but because I need to hear it.

Day Twenty-five/11:00 AM: You owe it to yourself to remove from your path all obstacles which might prevent you from realizing the new goals you have set for yourself. This includes self-condemnation, self-pity, guilt, remorse, and regret.

I make myself available for the next step.

Day Twenty-five/12:00 PM: It is only by telling our stories that we discover who we are. It is listening to others tell their stories that we are reminded of the truth.

I do "not regret the past nor wish to shut the door on it." (P 83, AA Big Book)

Day Twenty-five/1:00 PM: You are not your fault, but you are *your* responsibility. Others are not your fault either and they are *their* responsibility.

My behavior, my responsibility; your behavior, your responsibility.

Day Twenty-five/2:00 PM: Half measures do not avail us half, they avail us nothing.

Am I willing to go to any length?

Day Twenty-five/3:00 PM: You are responsible for what you think of you. You are not responsible for what others think of you.

When I play watchdog to other's thoughts, I remember that watchdogs have to bark and bite.

Day Twenty-five/4:00 PM: Do not be hung up on what

you ought to be, what you were supposed to be or what you were going to be. You will never have time to be what you are.

I am the best me there is.

Day Twenty-five/5:00 PM: "The world can only be grasped by action, not by contemplation. The hand is the cutting edge of the mind." Jacob Bronowski, *The Ascent of Man*

My recovery is grasped by as much action as my addiction is released with inaction.

Day Twenty-five/6:00 PM: Occasionally we get a glimpse of how others have truly seen us. It is a dreadful experience and if it weren't for the loving attitude of our fellowship, we sometimes could not bear it.

Growing is worth the pain as I slowly transform into the person I have always pretended to be.

Day Twenty-five/7:00 PM: Our recovery is not merely "not using." It is not just a program of "not doing" something but an action program where we must "do" certain things to maintain our abstinence and grow in body, mind, and spirit.

I enjoy becoming a human-doing rather than simply a human-being.

Day Twenty-five/8:00 PM: Some people do not *have to have* a program to stop drinking and using. But for us, we remember untreated abstinence will make our past our future.

I don't work the program to get my life back; I work the program to get my life forward.

Day Twenty-five/9:00 PM: The difference between Turing it Over and Rolling Over: To Turn It Over you say, "God, I know this is for the best, even if I don't understand the means. After all, I once thought it was horrible that I was an alcoholic and addict. Now it is my greatest blessing!" Rolling over you say, "Go ahead, God, and screw up my life some more. After all, you cursed me with alcoholism, didn't you?"

I turn it over, not roll over.

Day Twenty-five/10:00 PM: "We could never learn to be brave and patient, if there were only joy in the world." ~Helen Keller

My adversities are opportunities in disguise.

Day Twenty-five/11:00 PM: Fear is a darkroom for developing negatives. And negatives don't develop in the light of sobriety.

My fear faced is my fear erased.

§

Day Twenty-six/12:00 AM: When the pain of where you were is worse than the discomfort of where you are going, then you'll move.

The pain of my growth is a good sign, not a stop sign.

Day Twenty-six/1:00 AM: During times of stress, people get on each other's nerves and few are the very model of serenity or sweetness. When a tense situation erupts, especially during group conscience or general service meetings, remember that the eruption is a natural stress releaser. Before you react, ask yourself how HP would have you respond.

I lighten up by enlighting up.

Day Twenty-six/2:00 AM: Doing the next right thing in the face of a tricky situation is not a choice you can run away from. As the saying goes: Wherever you go, there you are.

I do the next right thing first,

so the "situation" doesn't last.

Day Twenty-six/3:00 AM: "We weren't perfect at it. Sometimes we rebelled, and rejected our sponsors' feedback or the guidance of the Steps. Still, the recovery process was always there when we needed and accepted it." (P 80, CDA First Edition)

I worked my using hard, so now I work my recovery hard.

Day Twenty-six/4:00 AM: Some days you will be shocked at how nasty and short tempered you are. You'll think, "This can't be me being so unreasonable." Yet it is. You may deny it's really you by jostling the blame on another, "If they hadn't...." No, your bad behavior is your fault. You have no excuse. Now, can you love you anyway?

I learn to love me even when I don't like me.

Day Twenty-six/5:00 AM: Whatever you need support with now: fear, frustration, anger, or boredom, try living in the solution, not the problem. Pick up your program book, close your eyes and leaf through. Run your finger down the page and wherever you stop, read the next three paragraphs. It's a random solution but often guided by Divine Presence.

A Divinely Inspired solution finds me now.

Day Twenty-six/6:00 AM: There are a lot more reasons for working the Ninth Step than freedom, serenity, and moral responsibility. Making amends is a good way of having the last word.

I take my program seriously and myself lightly.

Day Twenty-six/7:00 AM: "When one door closes another door opens, but we so often look so long and so regretfully upon the closed door, that we do not see the new worlds which open for us." ~Alexander Graham Bell

God wants for me what I would want for myself,
IF I had all the facts.

Day Twenty-six/8:00 AM: How important are the slogans? Sometimes, these are the only things we can bring to mind when we stand at a turning point, the thresh-hold of a crisis.

The slogans work much better for me when I decorate my life with them rather than decorating the walls with them.

Day Twenty-six/9:00 AM: As you begin this day at this morning hour, know that there are several million people who genuinely love you. This is the nature of our fellowship.

All the love I need is flowing into my life today.

Day Twenty-six/10:00 AM: Sweat the small stuff. The big stuff we can handle, it's the day to day crap that gets us. How do we attend to the small stuff? Steps Ten and Eleven.

Today I treat myself to quiet time in
order to review the small stuff.

Day Twenty-six/11:00 AM: Switching from one drug to another is like switching seats on the Titanic. If we try to say we have trouble with only one chemical (like pot or alcohol) then we do not yet understand the full nature of addiction.

Whether I call myself an alcoholic, pot head, cocaine
freak, or addict--I accept the far-reaching nature
of my disease, Chemical Dependency.

Day Twenty-six/12:00 PM: According to the martial arts, Akido, the best way to win a fight is not to be there in the first place. Think of this the next time you are invited to a bar, to ride in vehicle with a pot smoker, or to celebrate at the office party.

My best path to cease fighting anybody or anything, is not to be in the ring in the first place.

Day Twenty-six/1:00 PM: Positive clean thoughts of ourselves are a must. Picture yourself speaking at meetings, greeting newcomers, laughing, sponsoring others, and holding your head high. Clean and sober thoughts help counter years of drunk and dirty thoughts.

I picture myself laughing and sharing with others.

Day Twenty-six/2:00 PM: *Forgiving is not condoning.* It means you let go of the energy of condemning so that you can give energy to the process of good living.

God forgives "them" anyway, so I don't have to worry about withholding mine.

Day Twenty-six/3:00 PM: It isn't always enough to be forgiven by others. Sometimes you have to learn to forgive yourself.

God forgives me anyway, so I don't have to worry about withholding mine.

Day Twenty-six/4:00 PM: Is your ideal to be clean and whole? If so, ask yourself: What sort of neighbor is a clean and sober person? What sort of family member is a clean and sober person? What sort of Twelve Step program will a clean and sober person work?

Sober is as sober does.

Day Twenty-six/5:00 PM: The best tool we have for staying clean and sober today is *choice*. We can choose to hold on to past ideals or we can choose this new life. According to Webster's choice is: an alternative, an option, a preference.

The choices I make today, definitely affect tomorrow.

Day Twenty-six/6:00 PM: The death of the old and birth of the new is evident in all of creation. You can choose to fear it or revere it. Fearing the death of the old self is like the caterpillar fearing the cocoon.

I revere, not fear, the cycles of my life.

Day Twenty-six/7:00 PM: We make two great decisions in life: one, the decision to get clean and sober; the other, the decision to stay that way. Never make the decision *not* to stay that way when you are depressed or unhappy.

"Never cut a tree down in the wintertime.
Never make a negative decision in
the low time." ~Robert Schuller

Day Twenty-six/8:00 PM: There are many things you do not understand and this is actually a good thing. Can you imagine if you understood all that is? The reason behind every birth, death, tragedy, and joy? You certainly would not be content. Imagine a worm who understood all of mankind. He would not be happy being a worm.

I know all I need to know when I need to know it.

Day Twenty-six/9:00 PM: There are no magic wands or burning bushes in our program. Just footwork and faith.

As I feed my faith, my doubts will starve to death.

Day Twenty-six/10:00 PM: Are you reacting the way people expect you to or are you responding from your inner self? Acting "as expected" and not from your authentic self will only slow your growing process and interfere in your relationships.

When I accept you as you are and me as I am,
then we can be authentic friends.

Day Twenty-six/11:00 PM: You surely will be angry with your Spiritual Source at some point in your process of recovery, which in turn leads to guilt. You may not be sure it's "safe" to be angry with your Higher Power. It is, because God loves you just as you are and that includes your explosive emotions as well as the sweeter ones.

Nothing I do, think or feel can surprise my Higher Power. I am who I am.

§

Day Twenty-seven/12:00 AM: "Imagine if at every moment we each embraced the world as the gift it is: An apple is a gift; the color pink is a gift; the blue sky is a gift; the scent of honeysuckle is a gift. Hidden in every experience is a gift," ~Marcia Prager, *The Path of Blessing: Experiencing the Energy and Abundance of the Divine*

What is my gift right now?

Day Twenty-seven/1:00 AM: When you were born, you cried and the world rejoiced. With sobriety, you can live your life in such a manner that when you die the world cries and you rejoice.

My life is not a dress rehearsal.

Day Twenty-seven/2:00 AM: Reputation: what others are *not* thinking about you.

What others think about me is never as important as what I think about them.

Day Twenty-seven/3:00 AM: God *wants* to create miracles for us, if we would but step aside. It is when they do not occur that something has gone wrong.

Miracle: The unsolved mystery of my recovery.

Day Twenty-seven/4:00 AM: When working Steps Six and Seven we honestly have to ask ourselves "Do I really want to give up the defect? Or do I just want to give up the result of the defect?"

Being an alcoholic does not give me the excuse to act alcoholically.

Day Twenty-seven/5:00 AM: We may have empathy for

your situation but we will not pity you. We know that pitying you leads to you pitying yourself which leads to mind-affecting chemicals. Rather than pity you, if you need an attitude adjustment, it's very likely a fellow group member will let you know.

Attitudes are contagious. Is mine worth catching?

Day Twenty-seven/6:00 AM: Sometimes recovering people must do twice as much as others to be thought of as half as good—luckily this is not difficult. (P 167, Alkiespeak)

My success depends on me getting up
one more time than I fall.

Day Twenty-seven/7:00 AM: It is better to have someone sober and hating you because you told them the truth, rather than have someone drunk and liking you because you told them a lie.

I don't heap on the bullshit when the
truth is like Miracle Grow

Day Twenty-seven/8:00 AM: "There is never going to be any more or less God than is in every single face, event, or experience that comes before you. You must make a choice. What will you see? God, present in All, or separated loneliness?" ~Bartholomew, *Reflections of an Elder Brother*

Me looking for my Higher Power, is like
a fish looking for water.

Day Twenty-seven/9:00 AM: Honesty without kindness is cruel and kindness without honesty is co-dependence.

If I can't say it kindly, I needn't say it at all.

Day Twenty-seven/10:00 AM: "If we are too arrogant or too afraid even to consider amends to those we have harmed, regardless of their past or possible future actions, then we need to go back to Step Seven and learn a little more about humility." (P 64, CDA First Edition)

It's usually just when I think I have found humility, that I've lost it.

Day Twenty-seven/11:00 AM: The people you most need to give love to will seem like the ones who deserve it the least.

It begins with me.

Day Twenty-seven/12:00 PM: "…if an alcoholic failed to perfect and enlarge his spiritual life through work and self-sacrifice for others, he could not survive the certain trials and low spots ahead. If he did not work, he would surely drink again, and if he drank, he would surely die." (P 14-15, AA Big Book)

If I'm not working with others, then others will be working with me.

Day Twenty-seven/1:00 PM: A temper will get us into trouble and pride will keep us there.

I can't save my face and my butt at the same time.

Day Twenty-seven/2:00 PM: Listen, or thy tongue will keep thee deaf. ~American Indian Proverb

My Higher Power speaks to me through people. If I'm always doing the speaking, I'll miss the message.

Day Twenty-seven/3:00 PM: Our sober life-style calls for self-responsibility. Is there something you are committed to do this afternoon? Go to a group, go to a meeting, call a friend, or show up? You are responsible by being on time, keeping promises, doing what your sponsor says.

I am responsible for what I do, no matter how I feel.

Day Twenty-seven/4:00 PM: Never give up on anybody, especially yourself. For the only time you *don't fail* is the last time you try anything - and it works.

I never give up on anybody. Miracles happen every day.

Day Twenty-seven/5:00 PM: You may very well understand your demons, defects, compulsions, and fear. You have an arsenal of information about recovery to overcome them. Why then is it all so difficult? Deep inside you know what you always have known: knowledge alone is not enough.

I know that "no-ing" is not enough and "knowing" is not enough. I must do.

Day Twenty-seven/6:00 PM: We not only attempt geographical "cures" while drinking, but often while clean and sober too. When you make a move "for the better," unless you can *honestly* say you are running to something positive, then you are running from something that you haven't faced.

No matter how fast or how far I go, I can't outrun myself.

Day Twenty-seven/7:00 PM: Don't try to clear away the wreckage of your future.

I stay in today and forget about jumpstarting tomorrow.

Day Twenty-seven/8:00 PM: Each person you meet is in a specific stage of their life, a stage you may have passed through or not yet reached. Judging them by your standards and experience is therefore not only unfair, but could lead to unnecessary anger and frustration. (P 135, *Alkiespeak*)

I practice tolerance by putting up with those I'd like to put down.

Day Twenty-seven/9:00 PM: "Trust the Universe. Trusting means that the circumstance that you are in is working toward your best and most appropriate end. There is no when to that. There is no if to that. It is. Release your specifications and say to the Universe: 'Find me where you know I need to be.' Let them go and trust that the Universe will provide, and so it shall." ~Gary Zukav, *The Seat of the Soul*

I release my reservations.

Day Twenty-seven/10:00 PM: When you're being nice, it's OK to over do it. During the HALT moments, when you're too hungry, angry, lonely, and tired, it's not.

When I go too far, it is seldom in the right direction.

Day Twenty-seven/11:00 PM: In Step Eleven you can decide whether you want to feel God, hear God, or see God. Be specific. Chose one, and then, for as many moments of every hour of the day as you can, pause and look for It. Pause and feel for It. Pause and listen for It.

I seek my Higher Power everywhere, because that's where my Higher Power is.

§

Day Twenty-eight/12:00 AM: Not knowing, is not the problem. Not being OK with not knowing is the problem.

I don't need to figure it out. I just need to do it.

Day Twenty-eight/1:00 AM: "The significant problems we face cannot be solved at the same level of thinking we were at when we created them." ~Albert Einstein

When my problems are significant and my program isn't working, I work my sponsor's program for awhile.

Day Twenty-eight/2:00 AM: As we learn to accept our disease, our circumstances and what we must do to recover, we come to realize that although we may not have control over these situations, we do have control over how we react to them. Bill W., co-founder of the

Twelve-Step programs, wrote "We neither ran nor fought. But accept we did. And then we were free."

Am I finished with fighting?

Day Twenty-eight/3:00 AM: Eventually, in everyone's recovery comes the day when reason doesn't cut it and we hit a wall. At this point, you either have a break down or a break through. If you've been doing Step Eleven, you'll have the break through.

Sometimes I have to get on my knees to rise.

Day Twenty-eight/4:00 AM: "We don't see things as they are. We see things as we are." ~Talmudic Saying

I need to put things in perspective because
I have a disease of perception.

Day Twenty-eight/5:00 AM: When the student is ready, the teacher will appear. When you need to learn a lesson or gain an understanding, something or someone that carries the lesson will appear. It may be a relative, sponsor, store clerk, book, the morning news, or a dream. Somehow, the message will present itself.

I am amazed at the "God-incidence" of it all.

Day Twenty-eight/6:00 AM: "Drill your soul in right principles, that when the time comes, it may be guided by them. To wait until the emergency is to be too late." ~Marcus Aurelius (Emperor of Rome)

Sobriety is never an accident.

Day Twenty-eight/7:00 AM: Emotions are influenced by our interactions with others. How we signal others greatly influences how they respond to us.

If I am constantly being mistreated, I am probably
co-operating with the treatments.

Day Twenty-eight/8:00 AM: White lies, little lies, and unimportant lies are still *all lies*. Even small dishonesties will make your life uncomfortable. Is it worth it?

If I always tell the truth, I never have to remember what I have said.

Day Twenty-eight/9:00 AM: People may off handedly say "Have a nice day," and you don't see anything "nice" about today. Maybe they should say, "Have a nice day, *unless* you have other plans."

I don't "have" a nice day, I "make" a nice day.

Day Twenty-eight/10:00 AM: "Always be a first rate version of yourself, instead of a second-rate version of somebody else." ~Judy Garland

The only person I can ever be better than is the person I was yesterday.

Day Twenty-eight/11:00 AM: They say that when you are angry or resentful at someone, your best course of action is to pray for them. That's difficult when you'd rather bop the bastard. Say it like you mean it, until you mean to say it.

Whenever I want to get even, I get even worse.

Day Twenty-eight/12:00 PM: Sometimes it is heard around the tables that there's "us alkies and addicts" and then there's the so-called "normal" people. So-called "normal" people are simply people that you haven't gotten to know very well.

"Normal" is a cycle on my washing machine, not a cycle in my life.

Day Twenty-eight/1:00 PM: What lies ahead of you and what lies behind you is insignificant compared to what lies within you.

The thing that's so great about recovery today is that no matter where I am, I'm here.

Day Twenty-eight/2:00 PM: What you are feeling today

is not the way you will always feel. Happy or sad, mad, glad, or bad, the one thing you can always count on is that everything changes.

Even though I resist change, there's no way to progress without it.

Day Twenty-eight/3:00 PM: Treat your family like you would a newcomer. Give them the same latitude for mistakes, give them the same love, the same gentleness, the same priority and care. This makes for a well-nourished family.

When I ask "How can I be of service?" my family is at the head of the line.

Day Twenty-eight/4:00 PM: They say that Love is a verb, not a noun. How true we have found this to be. Love is also a principle that must be practiced on a daily basis. LOVE: Living Our Values Everyday.

My love isn't love until I give it away.

Day Twenty-eight/5:00 PM: Abstinence, honesty, and the willingness "to turn it over" are the only ways to fight the Four Horsemen of mind-affecting chemicals: Terror, Bewilderment, Frustration, and Despair.

The battle is no longer mine if I begin each day with the Third Step.

Day Twenty-eight/6:00 PM: "Laughter has something in it in common with the ancient winds of faith and inspiration; it unfreezes pride and unwinds secrecy; it makes people forget themselves in the presence of something greater than themselves; something that they cannot resist." ~G.K. Chesterton

I cannot feel sorry for myself and laugh at the same time, so I take my levity seriously.

Day Twenty-eight/7:00 PM: Probably any one of us can

get along with perfect people, but our task is to get along with imperfect people. The worst part of trying to get along with imperfect people is that they refuse to change into what we want.

When I think about how hard it is to change myself,
I know how hard it will be to change others.

Day Twenty-eight/8:00 PM: Your happiness will not exist in the absence of conflict or struggles, but in your ability to deal with them. Your ability to deal with them will depend greatly on your ability to turn to others for help. Do you have a Twelve-Step phone list handy?

"Happiness is pretty much independent of my
circumstances." (P 37, Meeting Wisdom)

Day Twenty-eight/9:00 PM: "...and in the act of helping, we ourselves stay clean and sober and growing. Therefore, carrying the message is vital. How do we go about it?" (P 81, CDA First Edition)

A good exercise for my heart is to bend
down and help another up.

Day Twenty-eight/10:00 PM: "I have made a pact with my tongue, not to speak when my heart is disturbed." ~St. Francis de Sales. He is not speaking about asking for help and sharing your troubles, he is speaking about leaving angry words unspoken when you are under stress.

Help my words stay sweet and tender,
for I may have to eat them tomorrow.

Day Twenty-eight/11:00 PM: "Always remember that each day as you look at your world and see millions upon millions of flowers opening up, God does it all without using any force." ~Dr. Wayne Dyer (P 91, *Everyday Wisdom*)

If I have to force the solution, then it's not the solution.

Day Twenty-nine/12:00 AM: On the way to becoming an old-timer, there are those who glow in their growing and those who are slow in their growing. The person who glows is always able to see the larger picture and the one who doesn't stays focused in their own little world. See yourself as a small part of a magnificent whole and do not see self as the whole.

The fellowship is not my whole world but my world wouldn't be whole without it.

Day Twenty-nine/1:00 AM: You cannot go back and make new choices or change the outcome of the past. But you can face the demons of your past and change your destiny.

Not everything I face can be changed, but nothing can be changed until I face it.

Day Twenty-nine/2:00 AM: The possibilities in this world are endless and abundant even when they appear impossible. Watch a tiny bird lift itself into the air by flapping fragile wings. See a pollywog transform into a frog, a seedling into an oak. Many wonders exist in God's world and *you are one* of them.

My Higher Power does the impossible, after I've done what is possible.

Day Twenty-nine/3:00 AM: Although selfishness, self-seeking, and self-centered resemble each other, there are shades of difference. Selfishness is: It's all for me. Self-centeredness is: It's all about me. Self-seeking is: What's in it for me? (paraphrased from *Alkiespeak*)

There is no limit to what I can accomplish if I do not care who gets the credit.

Day Twenty-nine/4:00 AM: Bernie Seagal said that everyone in life is broken, only some of us are stronger in the broken places. Ask yourself what makes you stronger?

When I pray for strength, my Spiritual Source sends me burdens so that I may build strength.

Day Twenty-nine/5:00 AM: It has been said that we are not human beings having a spiritual experience but spiritual beings having a human experience. As a dream is to your human experience, addiction is to your spiritual experience. When you awake, you realize it no longer has power over you.

Sometimes I need a rude awakening before I can have a spiritual awakening.

Day Twenty-nine/6:00 AM: Sarcasm is derived from a Greek word meaning "to tear flesh!" We know that the only weapon that gets sharper with use is the tongue.

I use my wit to amuse and not to abuse.

Day Twenty-nine/7:00 AM: We recommend that you take your Third Step every morning and turn your will over to the care of God, *as you understand God.* Then at night, take a Tenth Step to see how God is doing.

I talk often to my Higher Power. S/He understands better than most people.

Day Twenty-nine/8:00 AM: Just for Today; Day by Day; 24-hour program; Don't use today; Each Day a New Beginning; One day at a time; You can do anything for 24 hours; A Daily Inventory. The sooner you live in the now, the sooner you find freedom.

Living in the past, I live in regret. Living in the future, I live in fear. When I stay in the NOW, I am free.

Day Twenty-nine/9:00 AM: In order to forgive, you have to have blamed.

I don't have to forgive people, places, and things, if I don't blame people, places, and things.

Day Twenty-nine/10:00 AM: Don't think of a rabbit. You had to think of a rabbit in order not to think of it. This is why we must think of what we *do want* and not what we *don't want* because the mind energizes whatever we put in it, negative or positive.

I don't tell myself "I won't drink; I won't drug; I won't shoot up; I won't take a toke." I tell myself, "I embrace my recovery; I love my sobriety; I cherish my clean time."

Day Twenty-nine/11:00 AM: Want to know about your Spiritual Source? "It is a simple procedure to calculate the number of seeds in an apple. But who among us can ever say how many apples are in a seed?" ~Dr. Wayne Dyer, *Everyday Wisdom*

Even though I feel very small when the stars come out at night, I remember that I, too, am made of stardust.

Day Twenty-nine/12:00 PM: Before spiritual awakening...work steps, make coffee, carry the message. After spiritual awakening...keep working steps, keep making coffee, keep carrying the message. -Zen for the 12 Steps-

Enlightment is my ego's greatest disappointment.

Day Twenty-nine/1:00 PM: True morality is what we do when no one is watching. Growth is demonstrated by doing the right thing for the sake of doing the right thing.

I judge my growth by how good I am to people who can do nothing for me.

Day Twenty-nine/2:00 PM: Love is the ability and the willingness to allow those we care for, to be what they choose for themselves without insisting that they please us.

When I live and let live, I teach myself to love.

Day Twenty-nine/3:00 PM: You will be happy to know

that the universal law that created miracles has not been repealed.

I am a realist. I count on miracles.

Day Twenty-nine/4:00 PM: Do we stop loving a new-comer after they learn to love themselves? Of course not, but then they're not a newcomer any more, are they? Ain't the program grand?

I give it away to get it.

Day Twenty-nine/5:00 PM: Do not pay any attention if people accuse you of inconsistency. Of course you are! How else can you change? You cannot progress if you can't change and you can't change if you're always consistent. Practicing new behaviors is sometimes seen as inconsistent—be proud.

Practice makes progress.

Day Twenty-nine/6:00 PM: Some members believe that our program is too idealistic and doesn't really apply in the "real" world. They don't get the "in all our affairs" part. If it works in any place, then it works in every place.

If I work my program in only one place,
then I'm not working my program.

Day Twenty-nine/7:00 PM: Although there is a catchy saying that goes "You are not a human doing but a human being," we find in our fellowship that we must be *human doings* in order to *do* the program and cannot be immobile as humans just being.

What am I doing for others today?

Day Twenty-nine/8:00 PM: When we "cease fighting any one or anything," we must give up conflict. If you participate in it, you are part of the problem, not part of the solution.

Conflict cannot survive without my participation.

Day Twenty-nine/9:00 PM: "A boxer was in his corner on his knees praying, and someone asked a minister, 'Will that help him?" The minister replied, 'Not if he can't box." ~Fr Joe M., (P 105, *Alkiespeak*)

God works with me, not for me.

Day Twenty-nine/10:00 PM: "We can do no great things, only small things with great love." ~Mother Teresa

God does not want me to do extraordinary things;
S/He wants me to do ordinary things extraordinarily well.

Day Twenty-nine/11:00 PM: You must not force or *will* anything. This is called self-will. You must only *be willing*, this is called God's will.

Willpower tells me I must, but willingness tells me I can.

§

Day Thirty/12:00 AM: It is true that some people have caused us great harm. Yet those who have injured us have only done what they knew, given the circumstances of their life. Forgiving means to stop feeling resentment. Forgiving means letting go.

If I don't let go, I will lose my grip.

Day Thirty/1:00 AM: "Poor me, poor me, pour me a drink." We all know where feelings of self-pity lead. Do you feel the world has singled you out? Maybe it has, but not to pounce on you. We promise!

The world has not singled me out for pain;
the world has singled me out for progress.

Day Thirty/2:00 AM: Life is too short to spend it miserable. An excellent way to abate misery is to look at what you are blessed with. Unclench your angry fist, hold it up, and use your fingers to name five things you are grateful for.

(P.S. we mean now!)

Day Thirty/3:00 AM: If you think you are a victim of the universe, you are probably right. If you think of yourself as becoming whole from your experience, you are probably right.

I am the victor, not the victim. It took all of my past to make this person I love today.

Day Thirty/4:00 AM: Why wonder why? Why ask why? The "why" questions spring from only one place inside: self-pity. The questions to ask are the "how" questions. The right questions contain clues to the answers we need.

When I ask the right question, I get the right answer.

Day Thirty/5:00 AM: Step Six. "Many members mistakenly think this is a passive step requiring no action on their part, just words. Not so. It is just as much an action step as four and five. We act by *not* acting out and that is how we demonstrate our willingness in this step." (P 46, *Young, Sober, & Free*)

I stop any behavior connected to my defects. I do not take revenge, tell someone off, or procrastinate that project. Stopping the negative behavior is true willingness.

Day Thirty/6:00 AM: "The choice is up to you. It can either be "Good morning, God!" or "Good God, morning." ~Dr. Wayne Dryer, *Everyday Wisdom*

Choice, not chance, determines my day.

Day Thirty/7:00 AM: Our greatest strengths taken too far become our greatest defects and our greatest defects tamed, become our virtues. Wrongly used, honesty can become brutal confrontation, nurturing can become "I'll fix you," and consistency can become inflexibility.

I examine my Fourth Step list and see how, properly used, each fault becomes a feature I desire.

Day Thirty/8:00 AM: It's easy to see the difference between ourselves and assholes…, unless, at the moment, we're the asshole.

I have got to get out of my own way.

Day Thirty/9:00 AM: It is important to stay away from "trigger" people and places. Old influences can "trigger" an overwhelming desire to use: bars, pot smoking friends, raves, cocktail parties, dealers, angry relatives, liquor stores, heavy metal concerts, etc. We each need to determine our personal "triggers" and stay away from them.

If I hang around a barber shop, eventually I'm going to get clipped.

Day Thirty/10:00 AM: These are not the Steps we discussed, debated, debunked, memorized, or analyzed. These are the Steps we took.

I do not create analysis paralysis by keeping everything in my head. I bring it to my gut and do it.

Day Thirty/11:00 AM: There will be days when you don't feel well. Perhaps today is one. When you feel sick, even though you don't have a temperature or other outward symptom, you might have a *soul cold.* Soul colds chill to the bone and the best remedy is a good dose of Conscious Contact.

Belief without action creates cold in my soul.

Day Thirty/12:00 PM: Stop looking for the differences. People who matter, don't mind; people who mind, don't matter.

No matter my age, race, religion or chemical, I am more alike my fellow addicts than different.

Day Thirty/1:00 PM: "Fortunately, there "R" four ways to deal with "R" anger: Responsibility (Steps 4 & 5),

Remorse (Steps 6 & 7), Repair (Steps 8 & 9), and Repeat-*NOT* (Steps 10 & 11)." (P 97, *Young, Sober, & Free*)

I take responsibility for my own reclamation.

(adapted from P 107, CDA First Edition)

Day Thirty/2:00 PM: God does not work well under supervision but works great with a bit of gratitude. Express gratitude for the many gifts you're receiving.

I accept this "GIFT" from the God of my understanding:
***G**od **I**s **F**orever **T**here.*

Day Thirty/3:00 PM: The greatest fault of all is to be conscious of none.

Referring to my list again, I put out of my mind the wrongs others have done, and look at what my part is.
(adapted from the AA Big Book, P 67)

Day Thirty/4:00 PM: When you place your sponsor on a pedestal you are like a child bragging to the other kids, "Nah, nah, nah, my sponsor is better than your sponsor!"

I don't place my sponsor on a pedestal. It is only from a high place that they can fall.

Day Thirty/5:00 PM: If "I'll let the new guy do it," "I don't have time," and "They don't appreciate it anyway," are your major responses to people asking for help, remember: the recovery that was there for you may not be there for others if you don't serve.

I can't give away what I don't have, but I sure won't have it if I don't give it away!

Day Thirty/6:00 PM: People think that "nobility" is something special. But when you study the word, you come to realize that "nobles" were simply those who served the King. Nobles were servants. In the Twelve-Step programs, we are all nobility.

The highest office I can attain in our

fellowship, is Chief Servant.

Day Thirty/7:00 PM: "My basic flaw had always been dependence—almost absolute dependence—on people or circumstances to supply me with prestige, security and the like. Failing to get these things according to my perfectionist dreams and specifications, I had fought for them. And when defeat came, so did my depression." ~Bill W., *The Best of Bill from the Grapevine*

It is sometimes easier to understand that I should not do
for others what they can do for themselves,
than it is to understand others shouldn't
do for me what I should do for myself.

Day Thirty/8:00 PM: "Unless the medicine stuns you, it won't cure the disease." ~Zen Proverb

The easier and softer I find my way,
the less likely I'm getting the help I need.

Day Thirty/9:00 PM: You spend more time with yourself than with anyone else. Doesn't it make sense to put something into that relationship?

I am my own best friend and value
my own companionship.

Day Thirty/10:00 PM: Although the difference between someone clean and sober for only a few 24 hours and many many 24 hours is usually obvious, we do not all grow at the same rate. The only valid comparison is yourself to yourself over time.

It does not matter how slowly I grow
as long as I do not stop.

Day Thirty/11:00 PM: "As long as you live, keep learning how to live." ~Seneca

I teach others so that I can learn.

§

Day Thirty-one/12:00 AM: "An attitude of gratitude is simply practicing focusing ones thoughts on appreciating what one has rather than what one does not have." ~Robert Johansson, *Recovering Self-Esteem*

It's not so much that my glass is half empty or half full, as it is being dang grateful that my glass has anything in it at all!

Day Thirty-one/1:00 AM: They say the easiest way to stay clean and sober is to breathe in and breathe out and don't drink or drug in between. That leads to abstinence. Working the Steps leads to recovery.

Nothing is so bad that a drink or drug won't make it worse and nothing is so good that working my steps won't make it better.

Day Thirty-one/2:00 AM: The difference between self-love and self-conceit is very important. Self-love is a healthy appreciation of God's gift to you. Conceit is comparing yourself to others and finding them lacking.

I do not climb the mountain so that I can look down on others.

Day Thirty-one/3:00 AM: The process of healing will always involve you forgiving yourself first for your contributions toward a misunderstanding, and then forgiving others for not living up to your expectations.

"The meditation of my heart shall be understanding." Psalm 49:3

Day Thirty-one/4:00 AM: Emotional pain is not a character defect. It is a part of life and must be attended to like all our feelings. Feelings are not facts. They are bio-feedback on how we are doing today and what needs attention inside. How are you doing today?

Feelings won't kill me, but killing my feelings will.

Day Thirty-one/5:00 AM: Sometimes life gets extreme. Extreme actions and reactions can be frightening whether they belong to you or to others. Step back, breath deeply, and pray.

Everything can go wrong today and I am still OK.

Day Thirty-one/6:00 AM: "Approach each second with respect. If you move too fast, you miss the meeting point between mind and matter and become like the hare who scampered but lost the race." ~Unknown, *Pearls of Wisdom*

There is no speeding in the "trudging" zone.

Day Thirty-one/7:00 AM: Courage is more complex than spontaneous reactions to traumatic events. It may take courage to rush into a burning building or jump in a river to save a life, but they are almost instinctual. Sharing your deep feelings might be an act of courage far beyond gallant feats.

My courage is my fear in action.

Day Thirty-one/8:00 AM: You do not want your *prayers* to be mindless repetitions. Repetitions are for meditations where the goal is to still the mind. Prayer is *talking to God* and must be kept vital.

My conversations with my Higher Power remain vital because I talk to my Higher Power, not simply repeat words written by others.

Day Thirty-one/9:00 AM: "When adversity strikes, my message is always, Even this will pass...and better days than we have ever experienced will come." ~Dr. Norman Vincent Peale

I can't run from God, so I let God run me.

Day Thirty-one/10:00 AM: Divine Intelligence encourages us not to escape our every fear and tear, but face them, learning what they are here to teach us.

Fear knocked on my door...I opened it
and there was nobody there.

Day Thirty-one/11:00 AM: We say "love is blind," but *any* intense emotion can blind us. There is blind hate, blind fear, and blind faith, as well. Anything so intense that it shuts our eyes to all but itself, is not in keeping with our principle of open-mindedness.

I cannot be honest, open-minded, and willing if any part
of me is blind including, love, hate, fear, and faith.

Day Thirty-one/12:00 PM: Anger can be a source of personal power for people. Wrath is a way to try to control people, places, and things that aren't behaving according to our wishes. Although a natural reaction in us, it's *our* reactions that count.

I don't develop a working 'relationship' with anger.

Day Thirty-one/1:00 PM: Each time you cry "unfair" you are saying you deserve more. Do you forget so soon what your past really says you deserve?

It is Grace that brings me recovery,
thank God I don't get my just deserts.

Day Thirty-one/2:00 PM: Do you like being lied to? Didn't think so. Yet how many times have you said, "I'm fine" or "Everything's OK" when it's not? When your friends ask how you are, they deserve not to be lied to. When you lie to others, you lie to yourself.

I am authentic with others and thus myself.

Day Thirty-one/3:00 PM: Recovery is a period of metamorphosis. You think, do and react differently than you ever have before. You surprise yourself, disappoint yourself, and ultimately strengthen yourself, building your capacity to respond to futures quite different than what you dreamed about.

After I work the Twelve Steps,
the Twelfth Step begins to work me.

Day Thirty-one/4:00 PM: Addicts and alcoholics tend to be catastrophic thinkers. Each new obstacle is seen as disaster. A new debt becomes the first step toward bankruptcy. A confrontation becomes the end of a friendship. We have trouble not carrying things to the extreme.

Fear fuels my catastrophic thinking
and prayer fuels my inner peace.

Day Thirty-one/5:00 PM: When you are having a bad day, lower your expectations and start over!

The more I work on me - the better most people behave.

Day Thirty-one/6:00 PM: One of your greatest resources can be your pets. Animals are wonderful companions and better listeners. They give undivided and devoted attention--long past the time when others have exited. They do not judge and they love unconditionally.

I work toward becoming the person my dog thinks I am.

Day Thirty-one/7:00 PM: "Life is not black and white. Life involves the interplay of black and white. In other words, the gray area is where life takes place. A big part of the healing process is learning{and...} recognizing that life is not black and white." *Codependence: The Dance of Wounded Souls*

Nothing in my world is all good and nothing is all bad.

Day Thirty-one/8:00 PM: Some say that there are no "bad" meetings. Others add that if you've never been to a bad meeting then you're not getting to enough. In our experience, we come to understand, as in our entire life, the meeting is what we make of it.

If I don't hear what I need, I say what I need to hear.

Day Thirty-one/9:00 PM: Whatever vexes you currently, imagine for a moment what could make it worse. What can make it worse than that? Again. Imagine it, feel it, and come back to now. If you can make it worse, then you can make it better. Remember this: *you are not helpless* before your feelings.

I am stronger at what I'm doing, than my feelings are at what they're doing.

Day Thirty-one/10:00 PM: Whether you pray, petition, plead, protest, prod, or praise your Spiritual Source, whether you sing songs of gratitude or whisper words of doubt, this is prayer.

Got prayer?

Day Thirty-one/11:00 PM: Life moves forward. Your job is to move with it. The past is like a rear view mirror. You have to glance at it on occasion, but if you focus on it, you won't see what's right in front of you.

I look back at my past, but I don't stare.